TRANSITIONS

DEATH PROCESSES & BEYOND OF 11 ENTITIES

BOOK 14

VOLUME II

VERLING CHAKO PRIEST, PH.D.

Order this book online at www.trafford.com
or email orders@trafford.com

Most Trafford titles are also available at major online book retailers.

Print information available on the last page.

ISBN: 978-1-4907-6794-9 (sc)
ISBN: 978-1-4907-6796-3 (hc)
ISBN: 978-1-4907-6795-6 (e)

Library of Congress Control Number: 2015920231

Trafford rev. 12/08/2015

 www.trafford.com

North America & international
toll-free: 1 888 232 4444 (USA & Canada)
fax: 812 355 4082

CONTENTS

DEDICATION

I *dedicate Book 14 to the 11 Female Entities who came to me so sincerely to tell the readers about their death stories. May God bless them as they reincarnate back to Earth.*

FOREWORD

May 19, 2015 Tuesday. I have just launched the sequel to my previous Book 13. TRANSITIONS VOL.II *Death Processes & Beyond of 11 Entities* BOOK 14 will feature all women subjects, versus the men that came forth in the previous Book 13.

For you new readers, Jeshua/Jesus is my gate-keeper. He brings forth the subjects who have agreed to tell their death stories, entrance into Heaven, and to be interviewed by me. To keep anonymity for the women, I will carry on the code using the nursery rhyme Rich Women, Poor Women (versus Rich Man, Poor Man) and so forth.

Book 13 was well received and I am excited to hear what the women will have to say in this sequel. I hope you readers will enjoy BOOK 14 as much as I will in bringing it forth for you.

Blessings, Chako

INTRODUCTION

O5-19-15 Tuesday, 6:35AM. *Good morning, dear one; you are all ready to start our next book, TRANSITIONS Vol. II. Precious one, I am Sananda and I am coming forth now to present some of the questions you had requested that you could ask the Participants. You have asked the 10 subjects in the first volume their age and how old were they when they died and so forth. Now let us deepen the questions and hear more of their philosophy to show the readers more of what Heaven is at a deeper level.*

Adironnda said to ask them what form they were presently in. Since I am Love—my energy is Love—I wish to have you ask that question that I had asked of you: do you love yourself? Let us see what they do with that.

Then I suggest you spend time on their soul group, not the group process, but have they joined their soul group yet? That will show you their evolution.

Third question: what are they doing now? In the first book it seemed like the only one who was doing anything (on a regular basis) was subject #10 Military Man. He was flying and exploring, whereas the other subjects seemed to have no particular purpose. Therefore, I would like to delve more into that (dynamic). Now I will say…

Dear readers, most of you who have picked up Volume II of TRANSITIONS have read the first book. You have read the many types of deaths that people have experienced and their various reactions to their journey and how they reside in Heaven.

For you new readers, I am using the term *Heaven*, whereas it is more accurately called *Nirvana*. As you get into the progression of the soul, one will note that there are Realms. The person who has ended his or her life, either with disease or some type of accident—although there is no such thing as an accident—these subjects lose track of time. There is no time in the higher realms as you recognize on Earth.

For this continuing sequel I have brought women subjects to this channel. The first book had all men—male energy. Now we have women and the woman's viewpoint. There are hundreds of different ways that one can pass. It is understood for this book these Entities have passed and are having their Review where they get to feel and see the actions that they did in their years on Earth. Whether they were short years or long years, everyone reviews his or her life.

Some of the questions in the Q and A section will be similar to what we asked the subjects in the first book, but we are making the questions at a deeper level in order to give the subjects an opportunity to tell more of what Nirvana, Heaven, or the Realms are really like.

There is not too much more that I can say for the INTRODUCTION. It is pretty much what I said for the first book, so you might wish to go back and re-read that.

What I would like to do now is to immediately start this sequel and I will bring the subject forth. We are using the same code names for the clarification of the reader. Instead of the code name ending in *man*, it will end in *woman*. So it is not *Rich-man*, it is *Rich-woman*. Therefore, we will use the previous nursery rhyme for that makes the continuation from the first book to this one.

I will step aside now and let our first subject *Rich-woman* speak.

1 RICH-WOMAN

O5-19-15 Tuesday. I am so delighted to be here. Thank you for inviting me. I am the one with the code name of *Rich-Woman*. While I was not what you would call rich as far as monetary value goes, I was very blessed and enriched by those who surrounded me with love.

I was 46 when my contract ended as well as my life. This channel wanted to know what era the subjects were in when they died. To make this easier, my era was when President George W. Bush had his presidency (2001-2009).

I contracted the disease known as Multiple Sclerosis (MS). I was not given too many years with that disease. Some people can live 60 or more years. I contracted it when I was in my twenties. By the time I was 46, my body could not take it anymore. I asked to be relieved and I passed.

My passing was quite simple. I saw a hand reach down, and I recognized it as my dear father's. So I raised up and took his hand and he pulled me out. Therefore, he was the first Entity that greeted me. My Guardian Angel was there also and more or less stayed in the background because he could see that my father was counseling me— to know the ropes, we'll say.

I was one of those who did go through the tunnel, and I am aware now that not everyone does. It is a tremendous ride, and it is difficult to state just how long it took to get to Heaven. In some ways it seemed as if it went on forever and in other ways it seemed as if it was over very shortly. My father had my hand, and he went through the tunnel with me.

We came out the other end along with my Angel, and I was immediately taken to the Care Center where I was turned over to the loving Care Angels. My father said he would see me later. He kissed me on my cheeks. The Care Angels had me take my clothes off, put me to bed, and the wonderful Care Energy put me fast to sleep. I slept there for a month or more, healing the ravages of that disease from my body.

During my sleep, my soul took me to my funeral. I saw the various relatives I had left behind—my children, my husband, and friends. It was not a huge funeral, but actually, it was just right. I went to each one of them to say *hello* the best I could since nobody could acknowledge me. I was gratified to see just how many people were missing me.

The next thing I knew, I had come out of the deep healing sleep and my astral body was healed. I felt wonderful. I was told that now that all of those cells that had carried that gene of MS were healed also. Therefore, when I reincarnate, I no longer will have to have that disease unless I choose so—and I certainly do not.

My Angel then took me to my Review. I had a choice of how I wanted to review it—to watch it, to be a part of it, or to close my eyes and just listen. I chose to watch it. It was like watching a grand movie like *Gone with the Wind*. It went on forever—my life was gone with the wind. Of course, there were things I wished I had done better. I could have been more caring to people; I could have understood my children more—been less controlling. But all in all, I was what is called a *good mother* and gave to my family willingly.

From the Review, my Angel then took me to the Group room. I understand this Author calls this *Group Processing* and that is actually what it was like. There were about 40 of us in the room. The facilitator came in and talked with us and told us that on a soul level we were approximately equal even though some of us may be older or younger than the others in age. Even so, on soul growth and awareness we were fairly equal.

The facilitator had each of us tell how we had died. That was for the purpose of making sure we knew we were dead. And of course, now I am quite alive; although I reside in Heaven, I am quite alive, thank you.

After the Group Process, we were led to a Dining Hall where there was a vast array of prepared foods. We were told that we could come 24/7 to eat anything we wished, to drink anything that was available. Of course, all the drinks were non-alcoholic and there were no meat products. The food was delicious. I found I had quite an appetite. When you have MS, it affects all the nerve endings for the swallowing mechanisms, so that gradually you stop eating, as it is too difficult. You miss some of the succulent foods you used to love and could not eat. Now I made up for lost time and piled my plate with all the things I could not swallow when I was so ill.

From there we were told to pick a buddy, for we would be rooming together. We had a choice of a dormitory or a house with different rooms. For now, I chose a house with a roommate, and it has been a delightful arrangement.

I will now turn this over to this Author, for I understand there is a period of Questions (Q) and Answers (A). *Yes.*

Questions (Q) and Answers (A)

Q: *What form are you in now—astral or spirit form?*

A: I have dropped my astral body, as the saying goes. I am now more in spirit form. Therefore, I no longer require food. Since I was not into cooking in that lifetime, my focus is not on food.

Q: *So what is your purpose right now in Heaven?*

A: I have been assigned to help the little children. There are what you would call nurseries here, so as the little children pass, there is someone who will be a companion for them. You see, some little children take a life just for a couple of months or years to experience that and to teach their parents a particular lesson. So when they cross over, they are somewhat confused, and they need someone like me who will be a companion for them so that they can grow.

And grow they do. They grow very rapidly actually, until they no longer need to be in the nursery, shall we say. They go up through the different grades of school until they are able to re-enter that world of the soul. Each progression is a step up so that when the soul has died as an itty bitty baby, we will say, then there is that time when the baby needs to grow up again.

These little children are not just left on their own. There is someone with them all the time—not just an Angel but... Let us say the child died when he was only 6 months old or something like that. When he dies, he knows about a human mother, and so in order to make that crossing easier, there are people like me who can be like a surrogate mother for him until he starts growing. It is rather amazing. It does not take him a year to become a toddler, but he does need that balance, that love that is given to him. And that is what I provide.

While I am in spirit form, I can take different forms in order to be a constant balance for that child who is coming back into a soul form. I am able to shape-shift for him.

Q: *Please tell the readers about the animals, about the pets. How is that arranged so that they are reunited with their previous owners? Many of the pets had deep connections with their owners (although we know no one owns anybody, not even their pets), but that is how it is viewed on Earth. After the pets and owner have died, they want that connection again with their kitties.*

A: The kittens are in an energy band where the animals are. They retain their feelings for their owner. Their souls have blended with the soul of the owner, and they are notified when that owner is going to pass over. Then when the timing is correct, an Angel brings them together again and it is up to the owner whether he or she wishes to continue that relationship or is it more of a greeting and a letting go.

So there is an energy band that is for the animals. Yes, just for the animals, and of course anyone can go to visit. It is not like on Earth where the animals just sort of roam up and down the street.* They have boundaries and they recognize those boundaries.

Q: *All right, thank you. Can you give me and the readers any more of the little tidbits that you were not aware of when you first arrived in Heaven?*

A: Well, for me it had to do with religions. While I had my life, I went to church and we did the prayer before meals and things like that. However, I did not realize until I was with the facilitator in our groups just how far off from the truth that our religions were! We in that life were what you called *Christians,* so of course we prayed to Jesus and all of that. But in life, he was not that real to us.

In the Heavenlies, we find he is very real indeed, and when I was approached by an Angel to see if I would consent to be one of subjects for your book, I was awed to finally meet this Jesus in the flesh! It is an astounding experience. One is not prepared, I do not believe, for the unconditional love that emanates from this beautiful soul. He has colors that pulsate out from him.

You have spoken about the *mantle of greatness* in the previous book, which I have read by the way, and those colors emanate out from him. Each person has a different experience, but for me it was like watching a rainbow in action. Have you ever seen a rainbow walk (chuckles)? That is what it was like. He has a wonderful sense of humor and his eyes twinkle. You are engulfed in this love. So I wish to thank you for allowing me to come to you and be part of this book because the gift that was given to me to be in his presence is more than I had dreamed of, even thought of, and now it is a reality. It is pretty awesome.

Q: *We are drawing this interview to a close. As I did with the subjects in the first book, I asked each of them if they would like to ask me a question. Do you have a question for me?*

A: I kind of wondered if you were going to do that. I was trying to think, what I would ask this Author? What kept coming to mind, I guess, was how do you do this? I know you channel and you write the books, but how do you *do* this?

Q: *Well, that is almost like a hypothetical question, isn't it? (Chuckles). I love when I channel. I listen to people, what they are saying to me, and I type it up. It feeds me. It literally feeds my soul to connect with people and hear their stories; it gives me many blessings.*

A: I can see that, for your aura is so brilliant with many colors also. I do thank you for having me come. I am honored that in this nursery rhyme I happen to be the first subject for this sequel book. Thank you so much.

You are quite welcome, and I wish you all the best for whatever you are planning to do in the future. May God bless you in your new endeavors, and thank you for coming! This interview is now finished.

Sananda, I find it interesting that here is another subject who died of MS.

Yes, dear one, that disease ravages man and woman. All right, dear one, this is a busy week for you. We suggest not to strain your eye since you are still healing. So we suggest not sitting for hours on end typing away.

All right; thank you, Sananda. You are welcome, dear one. Your Book 14 is launched! *Yes, it is; I am so fortunate, thank you. Adieu.* Adieu.

*Author: I live near a golf course in Arizona and the coyotes roam down the streets looking for food—bunnies, cats, small dogs. I had one coyote chase a rabbit over my back patio and bump into a water drain so hard that it dented it. The bunny could not escape and was devoured. At another time, a coyote took a 2-hour nap on my cement patio. These Earth-bound coyotes obviously know no boundaries such as there are in Heaven!

2 POOR-WOMAN

5-23-15 *Good morning, precious one (7:30 AM), I am here. I am known as Sananda. You may call me Jesus, Jeshua, Lord, but I am your Sananda. We will be bringing in the second chapter of Volume II, Poor-Woman. I will step aside now; she has been briefed and knows what's up. So the next thought you will receive will be hers. Thank you, Lord.*

Hello! I am so thrilled to be here. I bear the code name of *Poor-Woman,* but that was not my lifetime, thank God. I understand we are to start telling the story of our death and our entrance into Heaven, and then there will be a Question and Answer period.

Yes, that is correct and thank you for coming.

You are most welcome! It is my absolute pleasure to be here. All right, my death... Oh, I am not very happy with that choice (*I made*). I know when we take a body, we make contracts of various ways we could die. I chose this one, and now I wish I had chosen differently, because it was a most difficult death. But let me go back just a bit more.

I was married happily; had a wonderful husband. I had children—a son and daughter. I did not like the fact that I would be leaving them.

I was what one would call a *daredevil.* I loved doing everything that a woman was not supposed to do. (I know that you, Author, want to know what era this was. It was in the early 1900's.) You know women were not ... They were looked upon as the lesser God. I was determined to show my neighbors, my friends, and my family that there was nothing lesser about me

Therefore, anything that came along I was willing to try. I was in the airplanes; I was in the fast cars; I was in the motor boats. I climbed mountains and skied, but I had not conquered my fear of deep water. I was determined to put on a (*deep sea*) diving suit and see what all the fuss was about. Of course, back in those days the suits were very cumbersome. You could not walk very well. It was extremely heavy outside of the water.

I hired this diving crew, for I was quite wealthy. I was determined to dive. I was not ready for the depth and the loneliness that could come over you as you sank deeper and deeper and the water became darker and darker. I had to really steel myself to keep from panicking, for as soon as I started to panic, of course, I could not breathe. The oxygen was being poured in according to the dials by the people who were manning the tubes up aboard ship.

I went lower and lower, feeling more and more panic. I had flashbacks, so I know now why I decided to risk all of this. I was actually trying to touch past lives where I had drowned. And we'll say, drowned I did! For some reason which is not clear to me, they say there is no such thing as an accident.

I was quite far down. I do not know how far but all of a sudden the oxygen stopped coming into the body suit—into that big, heavy helmet so I could breathe. I yanked on the lines and one of them came loose in my hand. I knew something was going on up on board the boat. I started really pulling on the lines and all they did was to keep coming loose until there I was standing in this rubber suit with this huge globe on my head and no oxygen (*holding the empty lines in my hand*).

I panicked and beat on my helmet and tried to jump in order to float up to the top again. Of course when you are that loaded down—your feet have metal in the shoes to keep you down and that heavy globe on my head was keeping me down. I could not screw it off; what good would that do? I would be full of water then. Therefore, I gradually lost consciousness and, of course, I died.

Now this is where it gets rather unbelievable because when I died, I felt this release. It was like I just popped out of that whole body suit. I just popped out! Here I was still under water. I started seeing fish. There was a man who seemed to be swimming around me. I later learned he was my Guardian Angel. I thought my Guardian might be a woman, but he definitely was a man—I thought. He spoke to me and I could hear him and understand him.

He said, *you are safe now, dear one. Take my hand we will go up to the surface.* So I took his hand, and he gently pulled me up through the water. I felt no pressure from the depth of the water. I felt none of that. I just glided right up. When I got to the surface, I saw my boat in the distance. The crew seemed to be scrambling around like a bunch of ants. I saw that there was a fire on board and that is why all the hoses got detached. I learned later that there was some type of accident, but as most of you know, there is no such thing as an accident. This death was planned very accurately.

I was only 25. I was in the prime of my life with a beautiful family and husband. I was not sure why this was happening to me. In fact I did not know until I had my review. But that is getting ahead of my story.

So my Angel brings me up to the surface and the water is not stormy. It is calm. Everything looked like one would want on a vacation. The sun was shining; the water was calm. The beaches were a bright white sand. There were no people. My Angel just kept saying, *you are safe now, dear one; you are safe. Come; hold my hand and we will go on a little journey.*

The next thing I knew, we just kind of whooshed out of the water (*chuckles*). I still don't know how they did that. Or I will say, how I did that. In my head I was thinking I must have gone through some kind of portal because the suction drew me right up into the sky and we just kept going. All of a sudden I saw this tremendous light and I was told, *you have arrived, dear one.* I said, *arrived where? How did I get here?* He replied, *we brought you through the tunnel and you have arrived in Heaven. That was your goal. That was the reason for your accident, although there is no such thing as you know.*

Of course by then, I was all bewildered. You know when your death happens to you and you are not expecting it, there is a time or state of confusion, because your mind is being asked to leave a 3rd dimensional world and be in the 5th dimensional world—these upper realms and what is also called Nirvana. It happens so quickly that you have no time to orientate yourself.

When I traveled—I was going to start saying when I was alive, but now I know I am alive and that was a death on Earth—but anyway, when I traveled and was on board ship, you would have these Orientation times and the lecturer would tell you about the country you were coming to so that when you got to the country you knew a little about it. You may not have known the language, but you were not completely overwhelmed.

But when you die, it is all so sudden. One minute you are on Earth and the next minute you are in Nirvana. You are so encompassed with such love—love I had never experienced even when being in the arms of my husband. I had never experienced such love before. It was completely unconditional love. It permeated every cell of my body. I could feel my fears dissipating. Even my memory (*of that life*) was not as perceptive as it had been.

My Angel took me then to what I now know as the *Care Center*, although some people may call it something else. It is a healing building. He took me to this and told me to get into bed. It was a pleasant room. What was surprising to me is I was stark naked and I had not realized that. Now I know I was in my astral body. I certainly was not going to bring that big, heavy diving suit with me! So I was stark naked. I climbed into this voluptuous bed. The sleeping energy of this Healing Center, this Caring Center, came over me. I went into a deep sleep.

I was told later that I did not sleep as long as some people had for I had no physical injuries. My trauma was in my mind. I had to reorient myself. There was this time when I was supposed to be in *acceptance*. That was a hard one for me. How does one accept the fact—living one minute, drowning the next—for our bodies were not made for that? When on Earth, *acceptance* was a psychological thing. It was difficult for me to accept the fact that I had designed this; that I had contracted for this. But so be it.

When I awoke, I was more psychologically fit. My Angel took me to where I would have my life's review. I later found out that my review was comparatively short, since I was only 25. But I did experience some of my youth that I was not too proud of. Since my parents were wealthy, I carried some of that, shall we say, stigma that wealthy kids carry, for they think everyone else is the lesser God. There is that arrogance, and hopefully they will outgrow that, but I was not given that time. So I did not like that part of myself.

My parents loved me. They thought of me as their beautiful daughter and had great hope for me with my marriage. None of that came true. I had a good marriage, but it did not last all that long with my death.

At the review, believe me, you do feel every bit of it. There is nothing you can escape. If you close your eyes so you don't have to see what you had been doing, you still see the picture behind your eyelids! So that doesn't work.

Then I went to this room where there were about 50 people, all of whom had died about the same time that I had. The facilitator came in and heard each one's stories. We all knew we had died by that time. We were congregated by the soul awareness. So we were all more or less on an equal level.

The facilitator talked about different things, making sure we all knew we were dead. We were a group of women, no men in our group. Other groups would have just men in them, for men carry a different energy, as I am sure you all know.

After that group—we were told we would be meeting every day for a while—we were taken to kind of a food court and shown and invited to eat what we wished. We were left alone for several hours so we could eat and chat with anybody we wanted to.

I was never a great eater in my Earth life. I was always watching my figure. I was so athletic that I was not prone to fat anyway. So I went to the salad bar and loaded up on very delicious fresh lettuces and vegetables. I did not eat meat even then. But I did enjoy seafood.

Then my Angel came to me and said he would show me my accommodations where I would be staying. He gave me a choice. *Do you want to be in a dormitory with a lot of others, or do you want to be more private in a house and have a house-mate? What would you like? Or you could have something like a hotel.* I said I would prefer in having a house-mate. So we went to this house. It was quite nice. It certainly was comparable to what I was used to at my Earth home. I met this other woman. She was just a bit older than I, but we hit it off right away. She became my house-mate. We started doing everything together and learned about each other's life.

Now I know you, Author, have some questions for me—sort of the Q and A part, since I do not know what else you would like to know.

Yes, thank you for your story. We have, Sananda and I, strived to have a diversity of how people have died. Therefore, the stories to me are very interesting.

Questions (Q) and Answers (A)

Q: *One of the questions I ask is, what form are you in now. Are you in an astral form or are you in a spirit form?*

A: I am still in my astral form. I was not ready to drop my body yet. It seems as if I still had things I needed to learn about that body. It was so athletic and did everything I wanted it to except the diving incident. So I wanted that body, for I wanted to practice deep-sea diving while I was in Heaven.

I know that might be rather surprising for people, but you can do anything you want in Heaven. If you are a race-car driver, you can have races with cars. I wanted to be a diver. I had lost my life in diving and in my fear. I wanted to practice with that body so that when I reincarnate—and yes I will—I will be able to dive. By that time they will also have better equipment. Therefore, I needed a body for that.

Q: *What was your purpose in that lifetime?*

A: I have thought about that. I think, and I am not sure, but I think it was to prove to myself that we as a human being can do anything we put our mind to. So many people put limitations on themselves and they are fear-based. They won't try things because they are afraid it might hurt them or kill them, which it can, obviously. I am an example of that. So I believe that was one of my purposes. You can do anything that you set your mind to.

Q: *Sananda suggested I ask the subjects some of these questions. So I am going to ask you, have you joined your soul group yet?*

A: Yes, I have and I was delighted to find that there were people in my soul group who were pure energy and there also were those who have kept their body like I have. I am finding, of course, when you are in your soul group that you study religions, for that is very soul-oriented. You learn the truth because in the soul group, it is for expansion and evolution. There are various gradations of it, or levels. I know lots of people do not want to say levels or dimensions, but in humanity, that seems to be the language that describes things for them.

Therefore, I will say that you learn to go up that ladder and graduate into different levels of thinking and evolving. But I, like some of the others in my group, am still doing that with my body. We realize at some point we will need to drop that body in order to advance to a higher degree (*of awareness*). But for now, our bodies are serving the purpose of being able to do anything that we put our minds to do with it.

Q: *Did you see any pearly gates or streets paved in gold since you have been in Heaven? Or has Saint Peter greeted you?*

A: I am chuckling because none of that, of course, happened. In my soul group, we have a big laugh about that. That is such an illusion. The Bible has many good parts, but *pearly gates and streets of gold* are such an illusion. Many people fall for that.

Q: *Do you believe in Hell?*

A: No! And I did not believe in Hell when I had my life on Earth either. That again is an illusion.

Q: *So what are you doing now?*

A: I do things with my soul group. We teach. There are always areas in Heaven where souls come in and need instruction. As above, so below. Some souls are younger than others, and they need to be led and instructed. They learn what illusion is and what truth is. As we in our soul group learn those things, we then are released and assigned different Beings that come from Earth and we teach them.

Some people in our soul group become facilitators for the new group processes and things of that nature. So that is what I am doing now. I am teaching, actually. It may surprise some people, but the facilitators for those groups are not in their astral bodies. They are pure spirit, but they have manifested a form so that they can shift their shapes—another shape-shifter.

In Heaven when you greet people, your heart is very open with the unconditional love, so you emanate this love. You reach out to all the new people who come forth to guide them and help them. No one feels put upon to have to do this. Everyone is doing it in joy. That does not mean there are not times when the newcomers need help psychologically. You see, everybody arrives with his or her, we'll call it, *baggage*. Those people need to retrain and let go of their baggage and understand why they were carrying it around. There are so many helpers, but they come from different soul groups. Say you have passed and are in an advanced soul group; then the helpers will be from an advanced group to help you. Everyone is kind of matched up all the time. There is always someone at a higher level. I do not want to say an authoritarian figure, but high enough so that you can go to that person and know that the answer to your question will be truth. It will not be illusion. It will be truth.

Q: *Another question that Sananda suggested we ask is, do you love yourself?*

A: That is an intriguing question, is it not? Because there are so many different ways one could answer that. I am not at the point where I could say I unconditionally love myself. I am moving toward that goal and there are parts of me I do love, but there are also parts of me that I know I do not love. Those are the parts of me that are not in integrity. So those parts of me I concentrate to bring love to—to retrain and expand and learn. So that is a loaded question that the Lord has asked us. Someday I hope that I can stand in front of him and say, "yes, I do love myself, Lord."

Q: *I am going to look over my list of questions and see if I have another question that may be a little different for you. Ahh, here's one. What was the procedure for your coming to me? Or, how far do you come into my field?*

A: An Angel of high caliber, we'll say, came to me. We started talking and he told me there was a person—he did not say your name—but he said there was a person who was writing a book that would be very helpful for man and womankind. It was about interviewing people who would tell their death processes and what it was like coming to Heaven, giving little bits and pieces of describing Heaven that people may have not thought about. He asked if I would be interested in being one of the subjects, as he put it. Of course I jumped at the chance, for I really enjoy doing things of that nature. I must say this has not let me down. I have been delighted. *Thank you.*

Q: *One of the questions that people have is, do you visit any of the people you knew on Earth or did not know—like play little pranks on them; knock books off their shelves or stop their clocks?*

A: No, a soul on a higher level does not play those games. There is no reason to attract attention to ourselves like that. Even after I died, I only visited my family the one time at the funeral. I was taken to that while I slept, which was sad because they were all sad. But I did not break any clocks to show them that I had been there.

Q: *One of the subjects said she had read the <u>TRANSITIONS</u> book already. So I ask you, have you read that first book?*

A: Yes, actually. It was suggested that I may like to read it and it would show me what the interviews would be about. So I did, and I enjoyed it very much.

Q: *Please tell the readers how you went about getting the book in Heaven!*

A: Well, there are libraries! As above; so below. You go into this building and there are millions of scrolls and books, and pictures. An Angel comes to you and asks what you desire, and you reply that you desire to read such- and-such.

At this point, the recorder ran out of tape and I decided to end the interview. 8:30 AM.

3 BEGGAR WOMAN

J uly 13, 2015. (7:25- 8:15AM) *Good morning, precious one; we are all set to do this once again; I am Sananda.* Good morning, Lord. I need to check you out. *By all means.* (I read a blurb and wait for him to answer that he truly is of the highest Christ Consciousness. Once he answers *yes*, I can proceed. Otherwise I have to wait, for the Entity may not be who he says he is.)

This is your third chapter and the Entity will have the code name of Beggar Woman, *although that is strictly a code and not a depiction of who she is. We will see what she has to say.* Thank you, Sananda. *You are most welcome.*

Hello to the Author of this book. Hello, thank you for coming. *I am so excited by all of this. I do not quite know how it will be, but I was told to just tell my story. And then there would be a Question and Answer period and to just go with the flow.* That is correct. Therefore, I invite you now to give me and the readers the story of your death and entrance into Heaven. Please be as explicit as you possibly can and descriptive. So take it away.

I have been here in Heaven for quite some time. When I died, I was quite young. I was only 35 or so. I have kind of lost track. The President was President Roosevelt (FDR). I had in some way contracted a disease that ended up killing me. You know that President Roosevelt had gotten polio and was quite debilitated. His legs were paralyzed, and he had to learn to walk using braces and crutches. Well, for me, I also got polio, but I died with it. When I had my life's review, I saw that it was part of my contract. It took me a while to learn why I set that up. What was the lesson I needed and was giving to my parents, family, and friends? It took me a while to come to grips with that and understand it all. But I am a little ahead of my story.

In those days, they had what was known as the *Iron Lung*. I was in this all alone and I hated it. It was like being encased in some weird machine and actually that machine was breathing for me. I did not look forward to the prospect of always being in that machine, for when the disease had progressed that far, you knew that you would not live all that long—or have a joyful life.

I had married by then, so all of this was going through my head. I did not want to leave my husband, for he was so good to me and I loved him so. I had two boys, and it still makes me sad. Every once in a while, I go to the great library here (*Heaven*) and ask the Angels to put my past life on the screen again, just so I could see my family. I am still in some ways attached to them. I do enjoy looking at them.

I guess you could say that I was kind of a guiding-Angel. I could not do anything when I saw that their decisions were not going to be very productive for them, but I held them in my love and I hope that helped. I saw them mature and grow and have their own families. It was difficult when I saw my husband find another woman, but after I had read my contract, I saw that it stated he would be married twice.

So there I was in this clunker. I couldn't move. The nurse took care of me—all the personal needs—the toilet and stuff. I hated every minute of it. I remember just praying these thoughts all the time, *oh God, please get me out of this. I can't take this for years and years. Help my soul leave this body.* I had said this repeatedly, and this one time, as I said this, I felt so dejected, and the next thing I heard was, *it will be all right, my dear one. You are out of that body and out of that mechanical lung now and forever.*

It startled me because I felt like I had two bodies—one was in the iron lung (I could see that) and the other body was me talking to this man. I said, *who are you?* He said, *I am your Guardian Angel.* I exclaimed, *thank GOD!* And he said, *yes, God heard your prayers.*

He then asked, *is there anyone you wish to say goodbye to?* There was nobody at the hospital I needed to say goodbye to, but *I would like to see my husband, my sons, and my mother before I go.* My Angel took me to the various places where my loved ones were. My sons were at school and my mother was at her house and my husband was at his work place. I visited each of those places. Of course they could not hear me, but I think my husband felt me, for he sat back in his chair and rubbed his arms as though he had goose bumps. He did not realize I was trying to hug him and telling him that I loved him.

I went to each of the kids and told them the same thing, and I went to my mother. Nobody, of course, could hear me or feel me. My Angel was by my side all the time and he said, *all right, dear one, shall we get on our way?* I said, *yes, I want out of here. What's next? Where do I go now?* He replied, *well, where do you want to go?*

You know, I discovered they (*Angels*) never answer your questions. They always answer you with another question! So when he asked me where I wanted to go, I replied, *well, I guess the procedure is to go to Heaven. I do not know where else to go!* He said, *yes, you're right; let's go.*

He took my hand, and there was this kind of feeling of rushing wind, but you still don't hear anything. I don't think I went through the tunnel. I couldn't tell you, but there was this rushing that went on for just a short while.

The next thing I knew, I was standing upright, and this place where I was at was in some garden that was just beautiful. I thought, *oh my gosh, I wonder where this garden is. I don't remember seeing this any place—this arboretum. I did not know where it was.* My Angel said, *you have arrived, dear one; this is Heaven.*

I said, *oh my gosh, look at this exquisite garden!* He said, *yes, everything in Heaven is magnificent. Now we need to get you to the Care Center so that your debilitating disease can be vanquished, and you can breathe like you are supposed to.* I exclaimed, *well, I am breathing now!*

Yes, but the cells are damaged and all of that needs to be healed. Come with me, dear one. He still had my hand and gave it a little tug. The next thing I knew, we were in this Care Center, and he took me into this sweet room—really a sweet little room. I always loved the English chintz. So here were these chintz curtains and bedspread. There was a comfortable chair. Everything was in a flower print chintz. Just like I like it.

The Angel then said, *all right, dear one, you have that hospital gown on, so slip that off and climb into bed.* I was kind of nervous, for here was this man telling me to take it off. He said, *I will turn around; just slip it off and get into bed.* So I was able to do that—took off that gown. As you know, there was not that much to the gown.

The bed was just absolutely perfect for my body. It was slightly warm and cushiony. There is this kind of energy that just wafts over you, so you feel sleepy. Before I knew it, I was in dream-land.

I actually did dream. I was at my funeral, I guess. It was difficult for me because everybody is crying and you don't think you are there. I was Catholic, so there was my body and I just looked like I was sleeping. My husband was just sobbing; my sons were sobbing; my mother was sobbing. Oh my goodness; with everyone sobbing, it is overpowering—the feeling of all that grief. I did not stay very long. Again, this was all in kind of a dream. The next thing I knew, I was back in this sweet room again. I woke up and the Angel said, *go back to sleep, dear one; you are not quite healed yet*. I did that—went to sleep again and during that time, my body was healed. I woke up again. My Angel was still there. I remember just stretching and stretching. I had on a green robe and the Angel said, *well hello; you are back*! I was not quite sure what he meant that I was back except maybe I am awake again.

Since I had my robe on, I flew back the covers and sat up. Then it dawned on me that I could move. Here I had sat up and had thrown the covers off me and there was no paralysis. I was breathing and just feeling so much lighter. You can't imagine how heavy you feel when your lungs don't work. They are just lying there, all paralyzed. Ugh, it just gives me the shivers, even now.

Anyway, it has been a long, long time ago since then. The Angel then took me to where the screens were. I never quite knew how we got there. It seems like if there is a thought of a place, you are there! I sat down and had to see the review of my life—you experience all the grief again, all the polio again, all the whole disease again! I made a vow that no way am I going to ever do that one again, thank you very much.

The Angel asked me then if I were hungry. I said *NO* since I had just reviewed that whole mess with the polio.

He took me into another place—a room or place—I don't know which. It was in a room with many other people who were all talking at once. It seemed to be the thing to tell how you died. People were saying this and saying that. Finally, this authoritative figure came into the room and… actually I could not tell if it was a man or woman. Come to think of it, the person was a woman—a psychologist or something like that. She started asking how we died. Each person told her story. I guess that was to make sure that everyone knew she was dead. There were no men in this group, so it makes sense that we had a woman facilitator.

We did not discuss anything except people's deaths, for the facilitator knew we were all kind of blown away with our review.

We were then disbursed; we could eat or we could be shown where we would be living. You know, we don't think of these things. I liken it to when we were on Earth and on vacation. There would be a discussion as to where we would be staying—at a motel, or at a resort, and so forth. And here our facilitator told us we would be told/shown where we would be <u>liv</u>-ing. That was kind of a shock to me. I did not think of myself as <u>liv</u>-ing there! I kept thinking I would just be <u>stay</u>-ing there; so that was a mind-set that I had to retrain, as they put it.

I had hooked up with another lady. We were kind of on the same wave length, and we did not want to just go and live by ourselves, so we said we would like to share space. It turns out one could live in a house with others, similar to a sorority house; so we chose to do that. It turned out the house was very nice. We had our choice of rooms. It had its own kitchen and a cook! We then had a choice whether we wanted to eat at the sorority house or we could go to the huge communal dining hall that was open to everyone 24/7. We ended up doing everything eventually, but at first we wanted to just stay kind of close to home, we'll say. There were probably 12 of us who lived in that house.

Some wanted to explore Heaven, so we…everyone had her Angel with her so we ended up just asking the different Angels. *OK, now can we just go any place? YES.* Nobody wanted to go by a smelly bus, so we decided on taking a train ride.

After that, someone else wanted to take a trip on an airplane, so we did that. So it was just like going to a big resort from one place to another. That was kind of fun. And then it got to the point of wondering what we were going to do next. Were we just going to travel all over the place or were we settling down? What were we going to do? That came up in our group discussions. The facilitator said we could volunteer for something. You see, no one is made to do anything. Everything is on a volunteer basis.

You could volunteer to be a teacher; you could volunteer to help in the infirmary. You could volunteer to be an apprentice to someone and to learn something new. So everyone was doing this volunteer stuff. I was kind of used to that because I used to do that then I had my Earth body.

I can't think if anything else to say. I was told there would be a *Question and Answer* period, so I guess this would be the time for that to happen.

Thank you for your story, and YES, there are questions that I have for you. I hope they are not too repetitive.

QUESTONS (Q) and ANSWERS (A)

Q: *You said you were around 38 years old and FDR was President.* YES. *Do you have a body form or a spirit form now?*

A: I am in my body form. I know some people have gone into their spirit form, but you see, when my body was so debilitated, it is kind of nice to have it again and have all the parts working. I am really enjoying it.

Q: *Did you finish your contract when you had your Earth body?*

A: Yes, that was very clear in my review. I was supposed to die when I did—give up my family when I did. That was difficult.

Q: *And you are going back again and be reincarnated?*

A: Yes, of course, because you can't have a debilitating disease like that and say, *OK, I am never going to have a body again!* It doesn't work that way. So I will go back and have another life. I was very much interested in the arts. I loved the piano and painting. I want to go back and be an artist, I think. Or I will say, try it on. You know, there are so many openings for you that you just say, *OK, next life I will be an artist.* But I refuse to be a suffering artist! I want to be an artist with money—have a family with money and let me be an artist. We'll see how that works out.

Q: *So have you joined your soul group? You can keep your body form, but have you joined your soul group yet?*

A: Yes, I have had that opportunity, and I have advanced to my soul group. The woman I hooked up with when I first came here and we lived in this house is also in my soul group, so maybe that is why there was such a connection that we just gravitated to each other and have done a lot of things together. When we were in the group process, it became clear that she and I had had many lifetimes together. Sometimes we were sisters or parents. We have had a lot of experiences together.

Q: *What are you doing now? Do you have some kind of a job with a title—maybe you are an artist already?*

A: Well, I have been studying art, that's for sure, and studying many different ways of bringing that artistic ability out. That is more or less for pleasure, but what I am doing as a vocation up here—everyone has a job. They won't let you…I shouldn't say that because everything is a choice…but after you have been here for a while, you don't want to just sit around. You are healed; you want to move. You want to do something. So you talk to your Angel guide, and he or she leads you to a work-match for you—what would be fulfilling. It is interesting that what I am doing is drawing illustrations for children's books. I know that sounds a little odd, but humanity has gone in another direction. They are not reading as much literature for enjoyment. I need to rephrase that. They are reading, but they are reading electronic books. They are not reading the books you hold in your hand. Therefore, I am illustrating those books for children. I find it fascinating that I can do that. I remember as a little girl there was the *Cinderella* book and then *The Three Little Pigs*—books like that. The illustrations are so adorable that I wanted to do this and bring out that fantasy in little children's minds.

Q: *Lord Sananda has asked that I ask the different subjects this one question: do you love yourself?*

A: Oh my, that is a deep question, is it not? That is so loaded, for it has so many facets to it. I could say YES, I love this part of me, or say NO, I do not love that part of me. But overall, do I love all of me or overall, do I hate all of me? It takes in all of those different ways of looking at yourself. When I was in the Iron Lung, I did not love me. But now that I am in Heaven and have this perfect physical body, I can say YES, I love me. But that sounds superficial, for am I just loving this façade? What's the depth of this physical body? What is the soul level? Do you love yourself at soul level? It is very complicated. So to answer the Lord's question…I have to think about this. I cannot just say from the top of my head, oh Yes, I love myself, for there are just too many facets involved. *All right, we will accept that answer.*

Q: *You know the Bible talks about pearly gates and streets of gold, St. Peter meeting you at Heaven's Gates. Did you see any of that?*

A: NO, and we all have had a good laugh over that, for that is just so made up by the scribes when they made up most of their religions. We are finding that most of the religions are not true.

Q: *So what dimension are you in now?*

A: I am still in the 5th dimension, but I am getting ready to take another step up the ladder. As you know, there are different levels in each of the dimensions, and I am getting ready to go up to the 6^{th,} so I am rather excited about that.

Q: *Please tell me the procedure for coming to me. How did that happen?*

A: A beautiful Angel with a gorgeous Light came to me and explained all of this. He just said he was an Angel on a mission and would I like to be part of this book? Of course it sounded intriguing to me, so I said, YES, count me in; I am all for it! *Thank you.*

Q: *Have you met many of your relatives who have passed on, and do they hold any meaning for you anymore?*

A: That is an interesting dynamic, for now that we know who they were, it is like meeting anybody on the street and hearing them say, *oh, I was your Aunt so-and-so.* Or, *YES, I remember; I was your Uncle so-and-so.* And yet you are meeting them in Heaven for the first time, and you don't know them. You end up just saying, *oh that's interesting.* Because you forget! When it has been that long a time, you forget that Earth life and those relatives, unless they were in your soul group. That's different. If they are in your soul group, that connection will stay; otherwise with most of the people who have been in your family or were school friends, you do not have that deep connection anymore; so you just let all of that go. You do not hang onto that. They do not have that meaning for you anymore. Let's put it that way. But, of course, my sons and husband are still alive in that lifetime, so I still remember them. My mother passed, and I still remember her, for she was in my soul group. So I still see her...I can't explain it (the feeling I am trying to tell you). It is like being with a group of people. You see them all the time. There is that connection, but there is not that real deep pull. Just like you know people in a group.

Q: *How about food; do you still eat food?*

A: I gave up food long time ago. We still like water, but we do not have to drink water. I like going to places where there is water, and we go swimming. There are waterfalls where the water is so pure that you can just open your mouth and have the water fall into your mouth. In that way we do drink water, but it is not a necessity, per se. Many of the people in your soul group are in spirit bodies, so they are not going to be drinking water and eating vegetarian hot dogs!

Q: *We have come to the end of our interview. I thank you. You have given humanity a great service, and this interview is now complete. You understand that you no longer can come into my space. Jeshua ben Joseph/ Sananda is my gatekeeper, so all Entities must come via his invitation. Again I thank you and wish you God's Grace.*

A: Oh thank you so much, great Being. I call you that because you just shine in brilliance. *Thank you.* I hope I can come again at another time, when I am needed.

Q: *Thank you again and bless you. Namaste.*

All right, beloved, that is Chapter 3. When you are ready for the next chapter, we shall do it. Love to you…

Thank you Lord and love to you also; over and out. (8:15 AM.)

4 THIEF WOMAN

0 8-10-15 8:15 AM. *Good morning, precious one; you are back in the saddle once again.* Yes Lord. I need to check you out. *By all means. Yes, beloved, I am the Christ. I am known as Sananda. Now the Being who is waiting to come forth is kind of nervous, for she feels she may not be giving you all that you wish. I will step aside now and let her come forth.*

Hello great Being of this book. *Hello yourself (laughs).* I am just so delighted to give you my story. I am a little nervous, for I am not sure if this is what you want or not. *Dear soul, whatever you say will be of interest to me and it will be part of this book. But do not be specific in naming any living or dead relatives and so forth, because I have to think of the legal part of all of the information. So please say what you wish and I am looking forward to it.*

All right, thank you. I have often wondered if everyone has a death that is peaceful for them or was it a struggle. I had an unusual death and I died with a lot of fear and pain. You see I was burned to death. *Oh my, that would be a painful death.* Yes, and I did not realize until after I had had my review that actually this was a way that my soul had chosen for that experience. But rest assured, we will not choose that one again! So let me back up and tell you about it.

I was, oh, probably around 10, before puberty. I had some friends over. That was during the time when smoking was considered very sophisticated. When you went to the movies, all the stars smoked and the women looked so glamorous. We girls would do this and think this was wonderful.

Everyone was at my house, and we found where the cigarettes were and the matches. We all took a cigarette and a match. We scratched the match and lit our cigarettes. The matches were still burning, and we were supposed to blow them out and put the burned match in an ashtray. I, for some reason, missed the ashtray. It fell off onto some papers that immediately started burning.

I panicked because there was no water around in that room. We started batting at the flames and all we succeeded in doing was spreading them. Before we knew it, some of the flames were on our clothes. Our hair was long and our hair caught fire. Most of the girls—maybe about 6 of us—most of them…actually, what they did was fly to the bathroom and turn the shower on and quickly doused themselves.

I was not able to do that—I and two others. Before we knew it, we were just a living, walking flame. We ran out of the house. But that did not help because the wind made the flames burn more and it was autumn time with many leaves on the ground. We could not roll around on the ground because the leaves would catch on fire, since we had tried that. Meanwhile, we were screaming and the pain was dreadful. I lost consciousness. I learned later that the other two were able to put their flames out and did not die. But the ambulances took them to the hospital also.

I did not die immediately; the ambulance took me to the hospital where I laid in the burn section. I was not conscious, so my thoughts were not there. However, I saw all of this in the review which made me ill just to watch it. I do not know if people realize it, but when you are having your review, it is just like looking at a movie of yourself. You experience every emotion, so you can feel ill and you can regurgitate.

But your Angels are there to help you. Even then, it made me sick to look at me.

The pain before I died was tremendous. They gave me morphine at the level they could, but you cannot stay on a high dose because you will become an addict. The dosages were just at a level to keep most of the pain from being too severe, but at the same time, my pain tolerance was not that high, so even with the morphine, I experienced much pain.

I was in and out of consciousness and I was praying for release. Since this was my contract, you see, I could be released. I experienced it all just so far and then was allowed to leave my body because I had had the experience for a certain length of time—several days.

After I was released, I was no longer hurting, but kind of standing outside of my body, looking down at this grotesque figure that was on the bed. I did not recognize myself, but I was so attached to it still that I knew it was me. I remember...you know, you don't know right away that you are dead. You just know you are praying for release and hoping to get out of that pain.

There was a nurse standing by me who I could talk to. She said, *all right, dear one, it is finished.* I said, *what you mean it is finished? That body on the bed looks dead.* She replied, *yes, dear one, she has left her body.* I said, *so where is she? Where did she go?* She looked at me and took my hands and said, *dear one, that is you!* It was almost like I lost consciousness again. I don't know if that is possible since I was already unconscious. How can you lose it again? So many questions...

I was in a great deal of shock, and this nurse was very comforting. She took me in her arms and held me and murmured sweet things to me. When I asked her her name, she said, *I am your Guardian Angel, dear one. There is nothing to fear now. It is finished.* I remember thinking how wonderful it is to have someone like her to help me—to be there for me. I thanked her so much, and I could barely move. She just kept her arm around me and supported me and said, *all right, dear one. Do you wish to leave now?* I said, *oh God, yes!*

At that time when I died, there were no relatives in my room. They had kept a kind of vigil around the clock and had just taken a break, so there were no relatives or friends there at the time when I died, except some nurses who were taking care of the body, who was me. So there was no reason to hang around. I did not know where to go or what to do. My Guardian Angel just kept murmuring to me, *you are safe, precious one; it is all right now; lean on me. I will take care of you.*

So with her arm around me, we just kind of floated out of the room, down the hall. I thought everyone could see us, but no one could. We were in a different dimension, so basically we were invisible to everyone. We just quietly moved on down the hall—kind of floated down. Then we seemed to be floating higher and higher.

I was in shock with it all, so I had my eyes closed and did not realize we had just raised ourselves out through the ceiling and into the open. I felt this kind of rushing of air, and I was so afraid that I could not open my eyes to see what was going on. I just kept them closed and my Angel had her arms around me, so I felt safe. She just held me.

Later I learned I was whooshing through a tunnel, but as I said, I did not open my eyes. I just clung to her; I was so afraid. One thing I did notice was I no longer felt the pain. I guessed that the morphine had really kicked in this time.

We kind of stopped moving and my Angel said to me, *all right, dear one, you can open your eyes now; you are quite safe.* I was slow in doing it, but finally I did. The first thing I noticed was this beautiful garden. She had taken me to a garden. I thought, *oh, isn't this lovely!* There was a bench there and we sat down. We were surrounded by glorious flowers and lawn. I could feel the grass on my feet, for I did not have any shoes on. I looked down and I still had that awful hospital gown on. There was nobody around, so it did not make any difference. We just sat on the bench, and she just kept murmuring to me and reassuring me that all is well now. *You are safe. You will be here many days. I am taking you to a Care Center where you will be healed of all your trauma,* as she put it, for of course, that body did not have burns on it, you see.

But my memory, my cells were all full of the burn incident, and they were distorted now because they had been burned. I do not understand it all, but that is how it was explained to me. Then she asked if I felt I could walk a little bit now. By this time I had calmed down. We were in this beautiful garden, and I just felt so loved. It is hard to explain, but there was such a feeling of peace and LOVE and it soothed me.

We stood up and she took me to this building and into this room. I was still kind of out of it, so it did not register all that much on my brain, except the room was very clean, pretty, and feminine-like. She helped me take my hospital gown off. (*Long sigh*). It still reeked of the burned tissue and stuff so I could hardly wait to get that off.

She brought me a warm wash cloth with water on it and helped me wash my face a little bit. I held out my arms and she helped me wash those too and my back. She gave me kind of a standing sponge bath. I did not realize it but she was taking energy that was no longer serving me off of me. She kind of tossed the used cloth toward a basket and it seemed to disappear before it got there. The Angel then told me to climb into bed now and rest. I felt so peaceful and did as I was told. I hugged her and thanked her and said, *thank you so much.* I got into bed. She helped cover me and before I knew it, I was asleep. Apparently, I slept several weeks but did not realize it.

Then I had that dream that everyone seems to have. I was taken to my funeral. I had not said yet that I was only around ten, so there were many relatives there—my father, mother, sister, two brothers.

Everybody was very mournful and crying. There were a lot of big flower arrangements. My name was on the flower arrangements. I was kind of confused too. Remember, this was a dream to me. I did not know I was actually there.

Everyone was saying I was too young to die. My friends were there—the friends who had played with the cigarettes and matches and smoking. These two others who were in the hospital with me were there also. Their hair was all burned shorter and frizzy. Their eyebrows were singed. Their faces were kind of scabby here and there. But on the whole they looked well enough.

Everyone was crying, so I kind of stood around because no one could see me. My Angel was there so I was thankful for that. She is the only one I could talk to. She said, *dear one, this is your funeral so say goodbye to everybody.* I dutifully said *goodbye* and with my parents I said, *goodbye and thank you. I am so sorry I did this. I love you.*

You see I had not had the review yet. I did not realize that all of this was part of my contract. My parents were to experience losing a child, for they had requested on a soul level that they needed to experience some emotional pain. They wanted to deepen their hearts and all of that kind of stuff.

Of course, I am saying to myself, *phooey! Know what you are asking for here (chuckles).* But when it is your soul wanting all of this for different reasons, this is what happens to you. So there I was saying goodbye to everybody. I felt more mature. I was thinking and talking in a more mature way.

So I said to my Angel, *let's get out of here. Enough already. They can't see me; I have experienced it. I have been to my funeral, so what else is there to do?* I was glad when my Angel took my hand and I was back in my dream world still asleep, which went on as I said for several weeks.

One day I woke up and felt wonderful. I noticed that my hair was again to my shoulders, wavy and curly. I touched my cheeks and they were all smooth. My eyebrows were back. I had had beautiful hands and they were like they used to be. It was almost like I was before I was burned—the pre-burn stage, back in time.

I was ten with that youthful body. I was considered very pretty and apparently that was all restored. My mind seemed more mature, and I knew more than when I was alive on Earth at ten.

So I was lying in bed stretching and feeling, sitting up and then I pulled back the covers and dangled my legs over the side. There were some kind of sandals for me, and I noticed I had on a green robe. I stood up and saw that there was a mirror and sink. I went over to the mirror and looked at me. You would never know that anything had ever happened to me. I looked just like I did before I was burned, but better.

I never thought that I was beautiful, but by looking in the mirror, I exclaimed, *oh gosh, I am beautiful—even prettier than I was.* That was true because I had had such a complete healing that all my cells were freshly new like the skin on a new baby. When I turned around, there was my Angel. She had on a robe also, having dropped her nurse's uniform—persona. She was now my Guardian Angel.

I just threw my arms around her and hugged her. I just felt so much joy; I was in such joy! I loved everybody and everything. I was filled with love. I said, *oh goodness, this is wonderful. What do we do next?* She said, *well, are you hungry?* I said, *I am famished.* So she said *come* and took me into a kind of little tea room. We sat down and I had some delicious tea and some buttered toast. That seemed to be all I wanted, and I did not realize that the toast was really full of nutrients. It was all I needed.

It was wonderful because when you are a burn patient, you cannot open your mouth wide. All food comes through a glass straw. It was marvelous to be able to open my mouth and know my lips were not burned off. I can't tell you how unbelievable it was to be so healed.

After a little while, she took my hand and said, *all right, dear one, this is the next step.* I said, *what's that?* She replied, *dearest one, you are going to have to review your life and see and feel it all over again.* I don't know if I could have, but I would have turned white as a sheet and fainted. I was just filled with fear and did not want to look at that burned body again. She assured me that she would be with me and it would go quickly. *But it needs to be done. It is part of your indoctrination to Heaven.*

Then it dawned on me that that is where I was. *I am in Heaven?* She said, *yes, this is Heaven.* I said, *I never quite knew what Heaven was, but so far I can say it is Heavenly!* So I said, *OK, let's get it done.*

The building, of course, was just full. I cannot express just how big it is. It was more like an auditorium, full of these huge screens. People were sitting in front of them. Some were sobbing; others kept their eyes closed so as not to view the screen, but the scenes just kept on playing behind their eyelids.

She took me to this area that had no one else sitting close by. There was a comfortable chair. There was a handkerchief for people to dry their eyes. There also was a pitcher of water. I was fortunate, because I was only 10 years old, so I did not have that many years to view and would not have to sit there that long. At 50 or 60 and more, the person would have all of those years to go through.

I sat down and the viewing had already started from when I was a baby, and I saw how I was. It went through those years and on to where I saw my school and my friends. I just went through all of that and on the whole it was OK. Then I felt myself getting kind of tighter for I knew what was coming up.

When my friends and I started to talk about finding some cigarettes and matches, I felt myself getting tighter and tighter in the stomach and knew what was going to happen. I remember turning to my Angel and pleading, *do I have to see this?* She said, *yes, dear one.*

I noticed whenever I turned away, the living screen would just stop. It could not keep going, for you would miss that segment. So it went on *pause* and as soon as I turned back and focused on the screen, it would start going again. I could not escape seeing that picture of me and that dreadful day when I caught on fire.

I felt that dreadful pain again. I reached out for the comfort of my Angel's hand. She held my hand and I saw the whole conflagration— the horribleness of it and being in the hospital and seeing that body, that beautiful body burned to a crisp so you could not recognize her. If I had not known that was me, I would have not known who she was. I felt everything. I understood what the doctors and nurses were saying. They were being very discreet and being sure not to say out loud what the patient might hear. But I could read their thoughts and saw the horribleness of it all. All I can say is it was a horrible, horrible death. And I pray to God that I will never go through that again. Never!

Then this screen turned off and my Angel and I just sat there for a while. She did not say anything, for I was the one who had to process all of that, you see. Those had to be my thoughts and not hers. I sat there for quite a while and was grateful for the cool water that was by my elbow.

After a while—my Angel could tell, you see, where I had processed to the point when I needed someone to facilitate more—to bring out more of my trauma. I was just to the point where there was nothing more to think about. By this time, my brain was just kind of looping, going over and over the same thing.

Then my Angel said, *all right dear one; are you ready to leave?* I said, *oh yes, I do not ever want to come back here again.* She smiled and said, *not for that lifetime anyway.* It dawned on me that when you have another lifetime, you will come back and do this again. However, I did not want to dwell on that and she did not let me.

She said, *all right, now we are going to join a group of people who are in a similar space emotionally and mentally as you are. These will be people who have died about the same time as you have. Some may be older and some may be younger, but on a soul level, you are all about the same maturity and the same awareness.*

She took me, I guess, to another building. You think of a place and you are there. I don't know how I got there, but the Angels seem to know how to get around. We went to this other building; it was just a short walk, but it gave me a chance to breathe in the wonderful air and the vibes. It was so peaceful and calm. I was so relieved that the review was over with. I said to myself, *all right, now I can get on with enjoying myself here. This will be an adventure; I was quite excited about it.*

My Angel took me to this room and I now know that this is kind of the *group processing* room. There would be a facilitator who would help people to talk. There were about 40 people there. Of course they were all women, but each one was kind of talking at the same time, telling her death story.

There were a few others who had a similar death to mine, so we kind of gravitated toward each other and compared notes. It was kind of amazing, for we did not dwell so much on the deaths as we did the review process. One woman was saying that she just regurgitated and now she was absolutely delighted she was healed. Eventually it would seem just like a bad dream—no, like a nightmare.

We all quieted down as the woman facilitator came into the room. She was delightful—another Angel, we found out. She had this authoritative demeanor about her, but at the same time, she was very caring and intelligent. You just knew that about her. She had us tell our stories. This seemed to take a long time because there were so many of us. It was interesting to hear the many different ways people had died. Everybody started comparing deaths, and we who had burned to death decided our death was the worst way to die. The facilitator kind of quieted us down as we listened to all of these deaths. Then she told us we would continue group tomorrow.

Our Angels told us they would take us to our accommodations. Interestingly enough, the four of us burned ladies all decided we would stick together—our own section in society—the burned society. We were given choices as to how we would like to live. We decided on the sorority-style house and program. We were taken to a house (*with several bedrooms*).

By this time everyone was hungry so we found the dining room. The long table was loaded with all kinds of food. We of the burned society all gravitated to where the fresh fruit was. Oh, the fruit was absolutely delicious. We had that with cottage cheese, magnificent rolls and breads. We had plenty to eat. We were told that there was a huge dining hall within walking distance for everybody that was open 24/7, but the dining room in our house—we called it our sorority house— was also available for us at any time.

I am trying to think what else you would like to know. I was ten and that would have been the era around 1950, maybe. I can't quite remember anymore. I can't think of more to say, Author. I understand there is a Question and Answer period. *Yes, this is the time I will ask you some questions—some I have asked the other subjects and some are new.*

Questions (Q) and Answers (A)

Q: *The first question I shall ask you is what form do you have now? Do you understand what I mean by that?*

A: Yes, I do. I still have the body, so I am not in spirit form. I chose to remain in a body because since I had died so young at the age of ten,

I wanted to experience a body longer. Do you understand what I'm getting at? *Yes, I do.* So I've enjoyed my body; it is a beautiful body, so I am just enjoying it.

Q: *Have you joined your soul group yet?*

A: Yes, actually I have. I have met them and we are joined in vibrations and awareness; so I do know my soul group.

Q: *Have you decided to reincarnate or not?*

A: I will take another body at some time. You see time is different here and it does not seem like it has been all that long from 1950-2015. It does not seem that long a time up here. It goes by so quickly. But yes, I will take another body after my Oversoul nudges me.

Q: *The Lord Sananda has asked that I ask each subject—if you do not mind my calling you a subject...* No I understand. *Do you love yourself?*

A: Oh boy—if you had asked me that when I had had that Earth body, I probably would have not quite understood what you were getting at. It wasn't in my consciousness to love or hate my body. I had an attractive body, so I guess I would say at that point, yeah, I loved my body, but put that on a superficial level. Here in Heaven, I'd say, yes, I do love myself. I am experiencing a new way of being and acting while I still have this body. It is similar to delving into its makeup and seeing how deep the memory banks are and how deep the heart is and all of that kind of stuff. And yes, I do love my body.

Q: *When you talked about reincarnation in your group, did you discuss how you would do it—be born again the natural way, or were you going to be a walk-in, or what?*

A: Actually that is in my contract from what I understand. I have not looked into that contract all that much, so I do not know all that much about it.

Q: *When you are in your group… Are you still going to your processing group?*

A: I am no longer required to go, but I go once in a while.

Q: *So did you find that you had to be retrained in your attitudes and beliefs and things like that?*

A: Well since I was only ten, I did not have too many—we'll call them *edicts*—that were cemented in. We were not a religious family, so my life was not predicated on religion. We were protestant. From what I understand, that makes it easier than if you were Catholic. In our family, we believed in God and that there was a Jesus.

Since I have been in Heaven, Jesus, himself, does visit Heaven. He comes to the different areas here and gives his talks. He appears— almost like the Bible says—on a knoll and He is surrounded by people and He gives a teaching. So we are still being taught. But this time we are being taught unadulterated truth. In other words, the scribes are not putting their input into the teachings and saying things He did not say or teaching things He did not teach. That is what I mean when I say His words are unadulterated. I do go to His groups whenever He arrives.

I was very thrilled and did not know that you are connected with Him, so that when an Angel came and asked if I would agree to be a subject for your book, I was in awe and astounded that I would be speaking to Jesus. Putting it in my words, you cannot imagine what a thrill that is. He is so revered and to think that I am a subject in—I am going to call it—THE BOOK that He and you are writing, it just puts me in awe!

Well, I can understand that. I am in awe, too, at times (chuckles). You are absolutely right. He carries that absolutely awe-inspiring energy, doesn't He? Yes, He certainly does.

Q: *Have you journeyed around Heaven since you have been there?*

A: Yes, I have. I want to say I might have died around the age of ten, but I am no longer ten. It is as if I have grown physically, mentally, and emotionally, so I would be supposedly in your Earth time, around 30, I guess. So when I journey around Heaven, I am not traveling like a ten year old but as a 30 year old adult. Therefore, I do have some wisdom here!

Q: *Thank you for the clarification for the readers. That is interesting. In that case I am going to ask you a more mature question and that has to do with intimate relationships. Have you or anyone you know of found a love partner? How does that work?*

A: Well, it is true that we can find a partner to be in love with and it is interesting to me in that I did not have that chance when I had my Earth body for I was only ten. But I have found a man who will be my husband in our next lifetime. We are already more or less setting up how we will come together and how we will be in love and have children. I can say yes, I do have a loving relationship and yes, we do have an intimate one. I am putting this delicately.

Q: *This leads me to the next question, because so many people want to know if there is sex in Heaven.*

A: I am giggling because yes, there is and it is amazing because it is so natural that one does not think of it being promiscuous, or anything like that. It is considered a normal process of a relationship—a precious intimate relationship—and yes, there will be sex! And yes, I have had sex and I have enjoyed it thoroughly!

Q: *(Laughs.) So the next question is—gosh, how can I put this delicately.*

A: You want to know if the sex is the way it is on Earth. *Yes.* And the answer is yes. It is a physical union between a male and the woman. The sexual genitalia is appropriate for that body and it serves the same function as it does with an Earth body. Both bodies climax, but the male body does not ejaculate because there is no semen—no seed, you see. We do not have pregnant women in Heaven!

Q: *Thank you, you are answering so many questions the readers will be wondering about.*

A: Now if you wish me to continue... *By all means.* When you are in your soul group and you are in your spirit body, there is no physical body. And yet there is still that intimacy of sexual drive and sexual feeling. This is from God Himself and there is nothing dishonorable about this. When you are in your spirit body, the coming together of the Light bodies unite and kind of merge into each other so there is this explosion, this magnificent explosion of Light, and that in itself, you see, becomes the climax. I have not had that because I am not in my spirit body so I cannot say more about it, but what I have heard and been told by others, it is quite wonderful and even better than the physical climax.

Q: *Thank you so much for all of those details. The readers will be very interested because there is not that much information that comes straight from Heaven that can tell us about intimacy.*

A: I can add that I have my partner at this point and he will be my husband; so we are having intimate times before we reincarnate and interestingly enough also, one does not have the same arguments here as you do in an Earth body. We do not argue. We can have different opinions and different ideas about something, but then we just discuss that. He tells me his opinions and I tell him mine. There is nothing particular to work out, for we know that neither one of us is wrong. That is all ego-backed psychology and we do not have this in a relationship in Heaven. You have your etheric bodies and there is not that type of ego. We do not feel we have to be stronger than the other sex or we have to be demure. There is none of that here; it does not make any difference. It never comes up because we feel totally equal, just totally equal.

I guess that is why it makes your relationship so precious because there is not that fight for one-upmanship. It does not exist.

Now for other people as they create a relationship with different partners and find they are not compatible, there is no horrible splitting up of emotions. It is like *oh, you think that way and I think this way. OK, it has been nice knowing you.* There is no fight about it and so that is what makes it quite wonderful.

And now since we have this personal relationship, we have decided to live together in a house. You want a house; you think a house; you got a house. If you wish to share a house with another person, you do. You can share a house with a male or a female.

There is none of that social stigma on any of this. Some people you know are meant to have a homosexual life. It is in their contract. They are meant to come to Earth and be what is known as a *gay man* and have a relationship with another gay man. That is in the contracts. The souls want that experience; it is all for developing the heart chakra. It is the same with two women—lesbians. That is in the contract.

Therefore, when these souls take bodies and are up against the heavy judgments and stigma that you get with that type of Earth life, it is a shock to them. Much emotional adjusting has to take place, for they did not experience any of this in Heaven! They were told this would happen and that is why their souls took this lifetime.

Humanity may scream at this, but at this point I would say that every person has changed genders in his or her lives. You come in as a female one time and come back as a male another time or vice versa. You change all the positions because it is a learning—a learning school on Earth. And boy do they/we learn! I got kind of carried away with this. I guess you can see I have a passion for this.

Q: *Yes, I am grateful for it because you have given us much information. There is another question I ask of you. Do you believe in Hell?*

A: Well since I was only ten when I died, that was more or less what people would say, *Heaven* or *Hell*, you see. So I did have that mindset that there was a Hell. And of course there is not. There is only the illusion of one which is all people's belief systems. I have not seen a Hell.

There are other illusions stated in the Bible—*pearly gates, streets paved in gold*. And yet you can meet people here even now and they swear they have seen those pearly gates and they have walked on those streets of gold. They will not accept the fact that those are people's belief systems that are not true. We find that very interesting.

My husband is a… I am calling him my husband already! My husband is a strong believer in people's rights to have their own religion and beliefs. So we will have an interesting life, that's for sure. And we hesitate in giving up what we have going for us in Heaven, as it is so idyllic. We eat together; we play together; we love together; we travel together. The thought of giving all of that up is a little intimidating. I guess that is why we are still here. But the time will come when we will have to make that decision. (*Sigh.*) In some ways it would be easier to come back as a walk-in, but then you are walking into what I call someone else's stuff! That stuff is not all that clean; it is someone else's muck-up! It is not easy.

Whether I want to take all of that on or not, I don't know. My lover feels the same way and yet we have to do it at the same time because if he's going to walk in to somebody and I am going to walk in to somebody, we'll have to choose people whose karma we can handle and find a way to connect ourselves.

And yet to reincarnate the natural way—oh my gosh, it could be 20 years before we could come together and get on with our life. Oh golly, it becomes a challenge up here; it is very difficult to make that decision. I guess that is when the soul says *this is our plan* and starts bringing people together and we work it out and set a date and we say,

OK, this is it. We're off! And then it happens and oh, what a jolt that is! So I am not looking forward to that part.

Q: *Well, dear soul, we are just about at the conclusion of this interview. I do thank you for all the information you have given me and the readers. I know it will be very enlightening for them. So I thank you so much for being so open in your discussion.*

A: You are welcome and I am so honored you chose me and I thank you!

You are most welcome, and I bless you and hope that you will have a wonderful new life with the husband you have already found.

I will now close this interview and thank you once again for coming to tell your story.

Oh, thank you, dear, dear soul.

Well, dear one, that's a loaded chapter for you.

Yes, that will have many dog-ears in our book. There is so much information that people have been wanting to hear—sex in Heaven—oh my goodness. It was very much needed and she was so articulate.

All right, dear one; it will take you a while to type up this chapter and finish the last one. I will speak with you another time. Much love to you, precious. I AM Jeshua ben Joseph.

Thank you Lord and it is 9:50 AM.

5 DOCTOR WOMAN

9-06-2015/7:25 AM. *All right, precious one; I am here. I am Sananda. Now we are to bring in Chapter 5 and another eager soul who wishes to tell her story. So I will step back now and let her have the floor.*

Hello, Author; I am a little nervous here. I understand I am to tell you my death story and my entrance into this fabulous place known as Heaven. *Yes, I and the readers would be very interested in anything you can tell us.*

Well, my death was kind of peculiar in that I did not know I had died. I was just fine—went to sleep and woke up the next morning. My family was there. No one seemed to talk much, but we were never a close family anyway. The next thing I knew... No, let's back up. I just went ahead with what I was going to do and read, meditated a little bit. There was one person I could talk to and she seemed to be able to listen and answer. That peculiarly went on for 2-3 days (*after I had died*)!

When I look back on it... Gosh, I can hardly believe this. You see, I had cancer of the breast and it had metastasized to the lung. I felt I could do the holistic healing and refused to take the chemotherapy and all of that stuff. So I thought I was doing fine. I had to take some oxygen now and then, but I would just go to bed and wake up the next day and do my routine. As I said, that went on for a few days. Then I started noticing that people didn't seem to know I was in the room.

There seemed to be a lot of crying and sniffling. My son was there, but I was not able to communicate with him. I started wondering.

I was into metaphysics, so I did know something about it. I thought, *gosh, am I dead? Did I die or something?* At first I said it like a joke because no one was paying any attention to me. So I said, *am I dead? No one is talking to me.* Then as I kind of watched, there seemed to be preparations for someone's funeral going on. Then it dawned on me. *It is MY funeral! They are talking about me!*

This one woman who seemed to come from nowhere and was always just there seemed to know what was happening. I asked her, *what's going on here? There is so much activity—people coming and going, telephone calls and flowers being delivered. What's going on?* She said, *you don't know?* I said, *NO, I am asking you!* She said, *it is for you, my dear one. You passed away in your sleep a few days ago and have not realized this. So I and your Higher Soul were just waiting for you to finally awaken to the fact that you are no longer in physical reality.*

Well, I must say that was kind of a shock because now I seemed to have a whole new set of dynamics to figure out. I replied, *well, how come if I am dead, I am still here?* I just asked all those kinds of questions. She was very patient with me. So I just kind of watched the activities. Not only had I died, but I was in on all the preparations!

So I just kind of stood around—but I guess you could say I just kind of floated around—and watched it all with interest. Pretty soon—you know, time is different in that reality—it seemed as if things kind of sped up. The next thing I knew, there was this Memorial; people were there. I noticed that some of my really close relatives weren't there. I wondered about that. I don't think they were ever told that I had died. So I just watched the whole thing.

The next thing I knew, my friend, who seemed to be the only one who could hear me and talk to me said, *have you had enough?* I looked at her and said, *yeah, I think so. What can we do now? Let's go do something different.* She said, *how about a trip to Heaven?* I burst out laughing and replied, *oh, that would be great—another adventure! OK, let's go.*

Then I was whooshing through the sky, so to speak. I don't know if there was a tunnel or not. I did not get that much into it. But my woman friend had my hand and we just whooshed through—I guess you would call them dimensions, or whatever—and it… In some ways the journey seemed very fast and in other ways it seemed like it took a while. I had no way of comparing in order to see how long it took, but anyway…the next thing…I couldn't see that much. I can't say it was dark, but it was muted—kind of like twilight, I guess you would say. You see, I was an artist, so I was interested in colors and things of that nature.

The next thing I knew, we seemed to enter this other place. It is like being in an airplane and you are coming in and landing at this airport in another country. We kind of made this landing, I'll say, into this beautiful garden. It was so exquisite in every way—little water fountains, birds flying around, flowers. It was just absolutely stunning. I remember just standing there and pivoting around in order to take it all in.

I questioned my friend, *is this Heaven or is this a way-station?* She said, *NO, this is Heaven.* I replied that it was absolutely exquisite. I could see now why when we are on Earth we use that reference—*oh, this is just Heavenly,* or something like that. Sure enough, it is.

The woman who was with me explained that she was my Guardian Angel and we were now going to go to the Care Center. The cancer was throughout my body and after being healed, if/when I reincarnated, I would not bring cancer into *that* body. That made sense to me, so I just sort of followed her. I did not know where I was, so I just had to sort of follow her.

She took me into this building. There were different floors. I do not know what the distinction was, but she led me down the hall (*on one of the floors*) and into a room. It was a lovely little room. I love color, so it was very nice. She told me to take off my clothes and get into bed. I did this and noticed I was tired. The cancer zaps your energy, so I was thankful to be able to climb into this comfortable bed in this lovely little room at the Care Center. What was interesting to me was that sometimes when I go to a hotel and climb into bed, it takes a while before I can fall asleep. At the Care Center you climb into bed and before you know it, you are asleep.

I asked my Angel—it took me a while to find out that my woman companion was my angel—*how come* or *why was it so easy to fall asleep?* She answered, *because there was a particular energy in the rooms that lulls you to sleep. The energy enters the brain and puts you asleep.* It is almost like an anesthetic—you are gone!

Now since I had already been to my funeral, I did not have that dream where people visit their funerals. I had just left my funeral, so to speak. While I was asleep for a couple of weeks, I guess, all of my cancer cells were healed. When I woke up, I was just ecstatic—I was in such joy. I did not have a large physical frame—maybe 5'4 or something like that. People would remark that I looked like Judy Garland so maybe that will give you a mental picture of how I looked.

I hadn't eaten that much when I had my cancer but I have my appetite back. *I would love to have some tea and whatever else you offer.* My Angel took me to a little café. It was in the same building as the Care Center, and people were sitting in comfortable chairs around small tables drinking tea. I always referred to that as *tea and crumpets*— wonderful, nutritious baked goods—muffins that were small and dainty. You take two bites and you'd have eaten one. (I always remember the *Sally Lunds*, those dainty muffins I used to make on Earth.) So I munched on. I then said to my Angel, *I need to brush my teeth.* She replied, *well, there is a rest room over there and you can go and you will find a toothbrush if that is what you wish.*

I went into the rest room and sure enough there was a sink and there was a tooth brush that was in a little box. I opened it and there was a toothbrush and some paste. I saw there were little paper cups over the faucets so I took one, brushed my teeth and rinsed real well. That felt really good.

I noticed there were no lavatories so figured they were in another room. But I did not have to empty my bladder so I said to my Angel who was still with me, *I have heard we always have this review of our lives. Is that what we are going to do next?* She replied, *yes.* I told her I had studied metaphysics and had read and heard about one's life review. I was interested but also kind of leery at the same time. I was not too good at experiencing new things. I would do it but had some trepidation about it.

We went into this other building that was absolutely huge. There could have been airplanes in there. But there was nothing but these large movie screens. People were sitting in front of them and there were all kinds of emotions, of course. Some were just sitting there very sullen and others were crying. You could not hear anything that was being said. Everything was very private. My Angel took me to a screen that was not occupied. Before I sat down, it had started playing. I watched my life from the beginning. I was an orphan; my parents had died and I went through all of that. It was so long ago. It was more of an interest than anything. I felt some emotion but it was not as traumatic as I thought it would be.

It went on through everything. I had several marriages and the review went through all of those. I saw that I was kind of ending cycle with all of these four men. They weren't always good choices, but I can see now why I had married them—karmic issues I was completing and things of that nature. I had a very close relative—a dear cousin—so I enjoyed watching our times together. (She is still on Earth.)

After the review, my Angel told me we were going into another area and there would be many people there. They all had died about the same time I had, and they all were more or less on the same level as I was, as far as soul awareness is concerned.

She took me into this room—they were all ladies. This was just for women, apparently. Everyone was talking about her death. There were not that many similar to mine where you just go to sleep and wake up not knowing you had died in your sleep. I guess it was the easy way to go after hearing the other horror stories. I just kept saying to myself, *thank God that was not me.* Even though I had the scary big C (*cancer*), the actual death was almost anticlimactic.

The facilitator came in—another woman. I could tell by the colors that emanated from her that she was a high Being. She had each of us tell about our death. I must say there were some shockers!

We were then told it was time to see our accommodations. We were asked how we wanted to live and rest while we were in Heaven. She gave us different choices—a dormitory, or a house to share, or something like a motel. What would we prefer?

I liked being with people so I said I would like a house, kind of like a sorority house with its own kitchen so I could go and make some tea if I wanted to at any time. We were each assigned our accommodation and would meet the next day.

Everyone who was in my house met as a group, and we went outside to the…hmm, it was not a bus, but similar. It did not have a top. We all climbed into that and it kind of rolled down the road. We saw other buildings and admired the landscaping and gardens. It stopped in front of this very attractive place. We left the bus and went in and were told to choose the room we wanted. Our Angels were with us. (They seem to just materialize in and out—there one minute and gone the next. Every time you needed them they were right there.)

I chose my room. They were similar to Earth's B and B rooms—Bed and Breakfast rooms. Each room was kind of different. Some were very modern and others had antiques in them. I grew up in this old Victorian mansion, so I liked that kind of old furniture and high ceilings. My room was like that—almost identical, actually.

We introduced ourselves again; we kind of knew each other from the orientation group that we had had. We gravitated to each other.

That is all I can say at this point. I was told there would be a Question and Answer period, so I guess this is as good a time as any. Is there anything else that you wanted to know? *No, and yes, there is a Question and Answer period.*

Questions (Q) and Answers (A)

Q: *Can you state more or less how old you were when you passed?*

A: Hmm, no; I don't remember. I was a school teacher and I had retired. So I guess I was in my late 70's or something like that.

Q: *Have you been assigned a job, we'll call it, since you have been there?*

A: Yes, actually. I am still working with children. I am helping them to bring forth their artistic abilities. I teach them what you might call *art classes.* Some of the children are more advanced than others; some draw while others are just in finger-paints. Therefore, I am still an art teacher.

Q: *Have you been there long enough so that you no longer eat food or drink water, things like that?*

A: Yes, that is correct; but I enjoyed baking so that whenever I want to, I will go to the culinary section that they have here and just bake something. There are delicious cakes—all sorts of things you can bake. I enjoy doing that. After you have prepared and baked something, you can eat it or dispose of it. It doesn't seem to make any difference one way or the other. The food just disappears if you do not want it. I think of it as being recycled whether it is or not. However, that is when I may eat—if I have cooked something.

Sometimes when I want to eat foods from different countries, I will go to those designated areas in this humongous dining hall: Japanese foods, French foods, Italian foods, American foods, Chinese foods, and I can experience those kinds of foods. Therefore, I may go there. It is not because I am hungry, but to satisfy some inner memory.

I do enjoy cooking, so I take lessons and learn how to cook this or that. I like making the breads and donuts. When I was a young Earth child, we did that in the family I was with. My grandmother made wonderful donuts. She had this pioneer way of preparing them. When the donut had finished frying, she would quickly spear it and dunk it into rapidly boiling water she had in a large pot on the stove. She then placed the donut on a wire rack in a warm oven to dry until she was ready to gently sprinkle cinnamon and sugar over it, or powdered sugar, or just keep it plain. When the water had cooled, she always took great joy in showing the family how much fat had been removed from the donut, making it a more healthy treat to eat.

To get back to your question, no, I do not have to eat. It is just when I wish to have a food experience.

Q: *Have you joined your soul group yet? Or maybe I need to back up and ask what type of form do you have now?*

A: I am in my spirit body, but when I want to cook something, I can manifest another body so I can have hands and such. But on the whole I am in spirit form.

Q: *So have you joined your spirit soul group yet?*

A: Oh yes, I have been with my soul brothers and sisters for quite a while. It was interesting to see that some of the members of my Earth family were in the same group—my aunt, grandmother, and cousin are all in the same soul group. That kind of explains why we were so close in that lifetime.

Q: *Have you traveled much since you have been in Heaven?*

A: I have traveled a great deal. I just love exploring—always have. I have gone to different areas all over Heaven. It is just like a world, similar to planet Earth. You can go to any place you want to—the mountains, the ocean, and the lakes. You are transported there, but it is always just absolutely exquisite, beautiful—5 star experience.

Q: *One of the questions that the Lord Sananda likes me to ask our subjects is do you love yourself?*

A: You know, I love myself a great deal. I am so happy with myself. When I had my Earth life, I always wished I were taller because my cousin was tall. She had these long legs and I wished I could have had those long legs also. But that is changeable up here in Heaven. My frame is taller, actually, and I am preparing my future body— what I wish—the taller frame and an artistic ability, similar to what I had had. Therefore, I have been training myself more. I take art lessons even up here. I have learned so much. Of course, there is this humongous library here and you can go and read the books. You can watch movies on the famous artists and I have done that.

Q: *Do you have any pets?*

A: I used to have a kitty-cat but I do not have a pet here, although a great many people do. You can get hooked up with animals you had in the past. I had this kitty on Earth but have not re-established that connection up here.

Q: *What about past relatives? You say you were orphaned so did you meet your parents and with the review do you understand why they died so early and left you so young?*

A: Yes, I went through all of that and yes, I did meet them. One of them is in my soul group and the other is not. We talked, and I understood the reason why they died when I was so young. It was all part of the contract. So yes, I have met a lot of the past relatives. I have told you it is different up here. I have had several husbands. I have met them up here and again discovered why we married and divorced. It is all the experiences and games a person plays when she or he has an Earth life.

What I found fascinating is that pull that feeling of wanting to be with a certain person is not here in Heaven, unless you were going to have another life with that person. Otherwise, it is similar to a high school reunion. You just say hello and you reminisce and you say goodbye. It does not hold that strong meaning for you.

I remember when I had my Earth life and people would discuss what would happen when you died and met your ex-husband. I can say now and give them my voice of wisdom here, don't worry about it. It will not be that important to you. There is not that pull. I don't know if that pull on Earth was purely sexual or what, but up here there is not that pull, unless you are meant to be together again. Therefore, husband and wives who are afraid they will meet so and so, I say don't worry about it. It will not be that important to you. It will not affect you that much—truly, don't worry about it.

Q: *We are getting close to the end of our interview and I ask everyone this, is there a question you would like to ask me?*

A: Actually, it is more of a comment than a question. I just wish to comment that *your* being able to telepathically do this and write the books is a wonderful gift to humanity.

I also want to add that when you wish to look up a past relative or friend, you can go to the library and dial them up. You then talk to them and decide on a time and place to meet (I usually choose the library.) and the person arrives almost instantly.

C: *Oh, thank you for that added information and thank you for coming and being a part of this book. I bless you and ask that you have a wonderful, productive new life when the time comes. I bid you adieu.*

Jeshua: All right, dear one, you have completed another chapter. Well done. Over and out, with love.

6 LAWYER WOMAN

1 0-21-15 7:10 AM

Hello, precious one! All ready to bring in another chapter? *Yes. I wanted to ask you, I have interviewed, not counting you, sixteen subjects. Are these all my past karmic people?* Some are; some aren't. Some are of your soul group and some are not. We did not choose just who you had karma with. We looked more at the subjects' progress and where they were/are in their advancement in Heaven.

Now this next subject we will bring in, of course, is a woman, and we will let her tell her story.

Hello, dear Author; I am so honored that you have chosen me and that I have been asked to be a subject for your book. I really appreciate this and look forward to it very much.

Thank you, and so do I. Therefore, tell me and the readers about your death and entrance into Heaven. You have a code name of Lawyer Woman, *but it is just strictly a code for anonymity. Do you understand?*

Yes, we have sort of been briefed on how the process will be. And many of us have read the first book, so we do know what we are getting into. *All right.*

I was quite old when I died. I had led a full life. I was a pioneer woman with my husband. We did not believe in divorce in those days, although, as I looked at some of my neighbors, it would have been better if they had. However, if there was discord with one of the partners, the person would just walk away. It was usually the man who walked away, leaving the estranged wife to care for the children. And usually there were quite a few children who were left behind.

I was out walking in my garden. I did have a garden and lived in the Midwest. I guess you would say I was a farmer's wife. I milked cows, fed chickens, churned and made butter, canned the fruits and vegetables. Most everything that people have read about the pioneer woman is true.

However, one day, I was working in my garden and I did not see this—hmm, it is hard for me to say it now—snake. It was kind of coiled in among the vegetables. As I reached down to pull a carrot— sigh—I felt the fangs of the snake go into my hand. I knew that was going to be the end of my life. I screamed. The men came running and with shovels chopped the head off the snake and helped me get back to the house and laid me on the bed, for they knew there was nothing more they could do for me,

Yes, they could cut around the bite; suck out the venom and spit it out. But I knew it was no use. I had yet to hear of one who could live through all of that. I just kind of accepted the impending death. My hand was immediately swelling. I could feel the venom flowing to my heart.

My husband called in the workers so I could say goodbye and thank them. He called in the children so I could kiss them and hug them and tell them to take care of their father. My husband gathered me up in his arms and just held me, sobbing softly, telling me how much he loved me and I told him how much I loved him. I thanked him for my life with him. Then I passed. (*I could feel her emotions and noticed the tremor in her words.*)

In the beginning, I told you I was old, but you see, I had not reached my 40's yet and that was considered elderly.

I remember lying In my husband's arms. The light kind of just dimmed for me. There was a ringing in my ears. The next thing I knew I was standing in a corner of the room watching all of this! I did not understand what was going on. I had had no metaphysical training. We were just dutiful Christians.

Everybody was praying while I stood in the corner saying, *God, Jesus, what's going on?* I frequently talked to him, just like I could see him, but never had. I became aware that there was someone else with me. I exclaimed to her, *did you see that? I don't understand. I am thoroughly confused here. I know that's me on the bed and that my husband is holding me, crying, but here I am in the corner of our bedroom. I am jumping up and down trying to get his attention and nobody can see that I am over here!* She said, *yes, dear one; you are in a different dimension now, a different level. You have passed, dear one.* I said, *you mean I've died? Yes, dear one; the venom took you quickly.*

I was in shock; it all happened so fast. (*Deep sigh*) I was just in shock. After a short while, the woman said to me, *would you like to go to Heaven now?* I just kind of stared at her. It was not the way one ordinarily would talk to anyone. I don't say to my neighbor, *do you want to go to Heaven?* Oh, golly! (*Chuckles.*) I was in so much shock that she was the one who had to make the decisions, as I just stared at her.

She said, *well, take my hand;* I took her hand. The next thing I knew, we were kind of whooshing through the roof of the house! I seemed to have lost consciousness or something. I was just stunned with it all. I remember just holding her hand and whooshing up. I was not aware of a tunnel. The light was kind of muted like it was twilight.

You know, when you die, there are those moments in time when your body is dying on earth time and you, the soul, are moving into

Heaven's time. So there is that period in there that is confusing to those who have just died. They are leaving something they remember and transitioning to something they don't know anything about but are trying to understand. So the woman, who I found out later was my Angel, is definitely needed. I think maybe that is why there are so many lost souls roaming around. They have in some way disconnected from their Angel; they are just confused Beings. I sure was. If I had not had the steady hand of my Angel, **I** might have been hovering around my old homestead. Therefore, my Angel took me up to what I now know is Heaven (*or Nirvana*).

There is another thing. Remember, back in those pioneer day, most of us did not have the education to figure out things philosophically. We did not have television or radios, so all we knew is what we could see with our eyes. I had a farm house that was kind of dilapidated and a barn. Our world was so small, yet so much happened in that confined space.

Then all of a sudden, you whoosh to Heaven, and you land, so to speak, and the immensity of it, the glorious, extravagant beauty of it can be VERY overwhelming. It impacts you so much that I can see now why your Angel hurries you right to the Care Center so that that energy can put you to sleep and you can heal from whatever killed you and at the same time restore you emotionally. It is too much!

Maybe some people would call it your *havingness level*. You are not used to having that space between buildings. Everything is so magnificent. We were used to having dust storms and dirt. Some of us had small gardens, but we had to be aware of snakes. One managed to get into mine and do its business—anyway... (*Sigh*). So I am glad my Angel took me to the Care Center and put me to bed. I had had it. I could not handle anything else emotionally. I was wiped out. It was amazing (*sigh*). And of course as you know, the pain was released from my body. Everything in my body was healed and made new like a new baby. My emotional body also was calmed down so that when I awoke a few weeks later, I could take in the magnificence of Heaven without being overwhelmed.

It was new and exciting, but I no longer had that feeling where it was too much—*it is too much; I am overwhelmed!* I did not experience that in Heaven once I was healed. I would say most everyone would not, for everyone is healed of that emotional impact.

Then my Angel took me to the Review building. I sat there and watched that ugly snake bite me. I tried not to even look at it and looked at my garden instead. But the snake was there. I could feel the fangs go into me and I jumped and grabbed my Angel's hand, and she said, *it is All right, dearest one; it's all right. That is just your death pain. It no longer exists. It is just like watching a movie.* But you see, there were no movies during my Earth time. I did not know what she was talking about.

I did not enjoy the review and heard that everyone has to go through that. I think one of the hardest things was to see my poor husband. Oh, I forgot to tell you that when I was asleep being healed, I did have a funeral, I guess you would call it. Neighbors came and I was laid out as the saying goes. People brought what they could spare for my dear husband. He looked just lost. I later found out that he married another woman who was a widow. She was younger and only had a couple of kids. Therefore, she was joined in with my family. So he had found someone to take care of him and he provided what he could.

Everybody was poor who lived on farms. One talks about the cities, but you have to remember the cities in those days were miles apart. Cities to you now would seem like backwater towns. The road would lead to a bawdy house, bars…

I did not stay long at the Review. After that, I did go to the group. Oh, there were a lot of people there who had died from snake bites. What can you do? When you live in the Midwest or the South, the snakes are there. Each person had a different snake story. Oh boy (*sigh*).

Then we paired up and most of us chose to live in little houses with maybe about five others so there would be six of us or eight of us. We needed to be with people. That is all we knew. We did not live by ourselves in mansions on Earth. So we returned to what we knew. If we had had a two room farm house, you did not have many wants. You were satisfied because that is all you knew.

So here I am in this small house with these other women. We get along fine and we cook food that we are used to and go to the group just for comradery.

Well I cannot think of anything else to say.

Well, this would be a good time then to have what
I call **Questions (Q) and Answers (A).**

Oh yes, I remember that.

Q: *Do you remember how old you were when you died?*

A: Not really, but I was not 40 yet, so maybe I was in my late 30's.

Q: *Since you have been in Heaven, do you have a new form or do you pretty much look like you did in your Earth life?*

A: No, I am in spirit form now. I dropped my body quite a while ago. I found it kind of cumbersome. I was no longer eating. By this time the group discussed how you evolve and drop your etheric body and take on your energy spirit body. so I found that is what happened to me. It just kind of happens. One day you have a body and the next day you are much more liberated and you look down and you no longer have arms and legs. It dawns on you that you have made that transition. So I am in what I call my *soul body*.

Q: *Have you joined your soul group?*

A: Yes I have and I am delighted to be with them. They take you under their wing. There is always someone who helps you make that transition, so you always have someone with you explaining things. Your Angel is still with you too, so yes, I am in my soul group. The six members of my house are also in their soul group. But we still maintain what I call my *farmhouse*.

Q: *I imagine you have talked about reincarnation in your group?*

A: Yes, we will all reincarnate, and it is getting close to the time when I will have to do that. We call it being *nudged*. I will soon be nudged to leave my comfort zone. I guess that is where it is a good thing when you go back to Earth and take another life you don't remember what you did in Heaven. That way you are just back into the density of Earth—Earth time and thinking like an Earth Being. I have not made up my mind yet whether to come in as a baby, the natural way, or come in as a walk-in. There are so many pros and cons that have been noted before. So I am still thinking about that.

Q: *What about pets? When you are in your soul energy body do you still have pets?*

A: I do not but surprisingly those that do… The pets, you see, can also drop their bodies and just be energy. Many people have their energy Being with them who was their favorite horse or their favorite dog. It is an energy body, and it is hard to explain but you recognize it as being an animal energy. So then you know it is that person's animal pet.

Q: *You have been in Heaven quite a while now; do you have what we would call a job—assigned some place to work?*

A: Work is a word, because what we do we do not consider as being work. We are learning something and enjoying it immensely. It is just fun for us. And yes, I do (*have a job*) and it has to do with my learning.

You see, I did not have that opportunity in those pioneer days. I had always wanted to know about things. So in Heaven, I study and then share at a pre-school level to people. I water it down some.

You could say I am a pre-school teacher, a kindergarten teacher, a high school teacher and then in between, I learn things too. It is fascinating to me for, as *above, so below*, the new inventions are being readied here. However, since I was a pioneer woman, I missed out on radios and television, so I thoroughly enjoy learning about all of that. If I were to reincarnate back into that era, I would be like someone coming from another planet, knowing all of this and using words that no one has ever heard of—smart phone.

They would not know what I was talking about—refrigeration—all of that. I learned about all of that since I have been up in Heaven. It is fascinating to me to know that you, Author, know these things—the computer, radio, TV, cell phone. All those terms we did not have; so it has been a joy for me to learn about all of that. And traveling... I think we might have had a bicycle; I am not sure, but a horse and buggy was kind of it. Now all the cars, trains, and airplanes have been created. All of this was not even in my imagination when I had my Earth life. It was all still being formed when I died. So there is that huge, huge learning that goes on and I could not believe that all of this had or was going to happen—the movie theaters—couldn't believe it. It was/is quite thrilling for me.

Q: *Thank you for all of that information. It is giving the readers a perspective to think about that maybe they had not thought of.* You are welcome.

Do you watch events on Earth?

A: Oh yes, all the time. Remember, I am the pioneer woman, so all of what most people do on Earth and take for granted is still just news to me!

Q: *So you can visit the Library and see all of this?*

A: Yes, and I had to learn to read, you see. I could read at a kindergarten level but I had to learn how to do all of that. That is why I went to school.

Q: *Well then, have you taken your first air plane ride?*

A: Oh yes, and it was quite wonderful.

Q: *Lord Sananda wants me to ask each subject do you love yourself?*

A: That's an interesting question. We did not have those kinds of philosophical teachings. But I can say yes, I love me.

Q: *Did you see what the Bible says are pearly gates and streets of gold?*

A: No, I did not have that illusion; we discussed that in group and were told that perception is all someone's illusion. We had a preacher man who came around our farms, but I do not remember his even talking about that.

Q: *We are coming to the end of our interview time. I ask everybody the same question—do you have a question for me?*

A: Hmm, I think it is more of a comment. I am just amazed that you can do this. Here I am up in Heaven; Angels have brought me to your presence, which is beautiful, by the way. *Thank you.* It has just been a wonderful experience and I hope you write many more books so that many more people can be a part of this. Everyone who has been a subject, as we get together and talk about this, has had such a good time.

Well, I guess it is different from being in a classroom where a teacher may be telling you that you have been wrong about something,

Yes, but that was not my experience either remember, so this is entirely different. And I will be talking about it for years to come.

Well, I do thank you for coming and telling me and the readers your very interesting story. I greatly appreciate your doing this for us.

You are most welcome, and I thank you again.

You are welcome, my dear one. When you reincarnate, I hope you have a wonderful, long life.

Thank you.

Jeshua: All right, my dear one. We thought that would be different for you since snakes are not your favorite animal.

Oh my gosh, no. Those pioneer days were very difficult, but one just learned to roll with the punches.

Have a good day! *Thank you, Jeshua. Over and out.*

7 MERCHANT WOMAN

1 0-27-15 Chapter 7 Merchant Woman 7:50 AM

Good morning once again, precious one; all set to bring in chapter 7? Yes. All right, dear one, I'll step back and let the person come forth. Thank you, Jeshua.

I am not sure what I am supposed to do, so I will let you tell me what it is you want.

Oh, thank you for coming; I am writing this book. Have you read the previous one?

Yes, actually (*It is available in Heaven's big Library.*).

So you have a slight idea of how this works. The readers and I would like you to tell your story about your death and your entrance into Heaven and what you are doing now.

All right (*long sigh*); I read about the deaths in the previous book and there were not any that I would care to experience. So I hesitate a bit to tell mine, for it will bring up all that stuff again. Oh, I hate to say it. I was a drug addict. Note I said **was**. Oh gosh, I had a boyfriend who was doing drugs and of course he wanted me to do it along with him, which made him feel like it was OK to do it.

I thought I loved him, but you know, at that age, it was just sex. I was young—only 16, for Pete's sake. As the saying goes, *not dry behind the ears*, but I knew better. I did not realize the pull that drugs have on you. Once I had taken it, he would have it ready for the next time. We both would get high. Oh (*sigh*), it became a pattern. Then I was hooked.

Of course, I had no money. The little he had, he had stolen. So after a while he got tired of supporting *my habit*, he called it and just left. Here I am 16 with no money, homeless. I used to crawl into doorways to keep warm. This was in the San Francisco area. You just kind of joined all the other addicts.

In order to get money, I would go into the areas where men were seeking sex and I sold that for money. Then I went and bought the drugs (*sigh*) and gradually upped my craving. You name it; I had done it. I see, Author, you have never done drugs in your entire life. I bless you for that. But it was an experience—a learning experience for me. Therefore, it was not too long of course, a year or more, when I overdosed.

Why I never got pregnant, I haven't the slightest idea. Sometimes the guys would use a condom and other times they were in just too much of a hurry and really didn't give a darn. They knew they would never see me again anyway and if they sowed their seed and it sprang forth, they would not know about it. You see they had had so many women, they really did not know (*if any became pregnant from their seed*). So I overdosed. It was quite a while ago. President Nixon was in office, and there was that mess with Watergate (*1969-1974*).

So there I was in a doorway, and I just remember I kind of blacked out. The other times when I had blacked out, I would come to. This time I didn't. The next thing I knew, I was standing over my body, jiggling it with my foot trying to get some life going back into it. Of course, that did not work.

There was this other woman who was very nice. I thought she was just a pedestrian or something like that. Later on I learned she was my *Guardian Angel*; but anyway, she came up to me and asked me if I needed some help. Of course, I was just staring at her, as I did not understand what was going on. She said, *come, dear one; it is finished.* I was still in shock, so I just took the hand she had offered me and we just floated away from the scene. Later on, I saw the scene in my Review but I will talk about that later.

I didn't question too much. I just took her hand. At that point I think I was still kind of in that drug mode. Lots of time you are just used to having someone take your arm and shove you some place or take you some place because you do not know what the heck you are doing. So when she held out her hand to me, I just took it—sort of grasped it— and just followed her. As I say, I seemed to be just floating. I oriented just a bit and asked, *where are you taking me?* She replied. *We're going to Heaven.* That did not sink in yet, you see. I was in that mode of confusion. I did not recognize the fact that my body was lying there dead. It was more like it was just asleep. I did not quite know what I was doing. I was not in the body, so when she said we were going to Heaven, that was a shock too. I did not say much.

So we whooshed to Heaven. I think it must have been through the tunnel I had heard about and read about. I just closed my eyes and let it happen. It seemed like we were whooshing for quite a while. I was half asleep. It was like being in an airplane, although this time there was no plane.

We landed and the next thing I knew, she said, *you can open your eyes now, dear one. We are here.* I opened my eyes and was absolutely astonished at the beauty that surrounded me. It had been a long time since I had seen lush gardens and flowers, butterflies, beautiful birds singing. Everything that most people have dreamed about in a spectacular movie was there—just extraordinary.

We landed, so to speak. My Angel then said to me, *all right dear one, we are going to go to the Care Center, for your body has been ravaged by drugs and you need to be healed.* I knew I was ravaged but did not know I could be healed. I had tried that on Earth and it had not worked. But I had not had the will power to stop using either. Therefore, I just followed her and she took me to this building into this room—this nice little room. Then she told me to undress. My clothes were pretty bad by then, smelly, and I needed to bathe, wash my hair. She assured me that all that would be taken care of. *Just undress and climb into bed.* I did what I was told and as soon as I hit the pillow, I was asleep.

I had a weird dream and was told later that I had been at what would have been a memorial or funeral. But I had not had one. It was just the city finding my body and taking it to the morgue and everything else that was involved—the medical examiner knew right away what had caused my death. They drew some blood and saw the drugs, so I just became a *Jane Doe.* I was buried in an area—sort of like the unmarked grave area. I was not cremated. I know they do cremate some of the bodies, but not mine. So that was more or less my funeral.

I was to watch that in order to see what had happened to my body. I had had a family, but I was a run-away at that point; so I don't think my family knew where I was or cared. That was almost like it was when I left, *whew, I'm glad she's gone!* It was an interesting life that my soul had chosen.

Therefore (*long sigh*), I slept for several weeks and was healed. When I awoke, my Angel was there. I stretched and sat up and exclaimed, *oh, I feel so good! I feel wonderful.* I had clarity of mind and memory. I remembered that life—remembered what it was like to be so drugged. Now the feeling of being so cleared out of all of that drug-fog...I felt so refreshed and healthy and felt like I could run around a block.

Then my Angel took me to a little room and offered me some tea and a light breakfast. I found I was ravenous, so right there almost without ordering it, the food arrived. I had only thought about it and there it was. My favorite was French toast, and there it was with fresh-squeezed orange juice. Ah, it was Heavenly, but I was in Heaven! It was perfect.

From there we went to see my Review. Hmm, what a sad place that is. Of course it is huge, like an airplane hangar, nothing but huge viewing screens but they had comfortable chairs. It was furnished well with carpet on the floor. I guess I was just picking up the vibes. It was so sad. I do not think—I don't know, since I have not been there that I can remember—but I don't think there was anyone there who was delighted in what they were viewing of their past life.

I sat and viewed my 16 years. Of course, it was pretty horrible, oh (*long sigh*), and I experienced the lethargy of being on those drugs; I just kept saying to myself, *what did I find that was so wonderful about all of that*. It was **horrible**—ugh! And I hated every minute of viewing it. I could not believe that I had done that to myself. I would say that to my Angel, and she replied, *that is one of the first steps to healing, is it not?* Ah, never again, never again!

From there we went to the Group Processing area. There were about 60 people, I guess. I did not count them, but it was a crowded room. All had died from drugs. *Incredible,* I thought, as I looked at them. Everybody had on different colored robes. Mine was green. I guess that was for healing. We all were kind of sizing each other up. We were all women; it was crowded enough so you kind of bumped into people. It got to the point when we did not talk about our deaths. We were all druggies. It was an interesting feeling.

Then the facilitator came in and asked each one of us to tell how we had died. Boy, if that wasn't an eye opener. I could not believe the variety of things that had happened to them. Of course, they had all been drugged (*either by their own hand or someone else's*). Some had been killed while they were drugged; others had been raped while they were drugged, some killed themselves by over-dosing. That was my category. Oh, it was awful. We sat there the whole time listening to everyone's story. I was so inundated with that experience that I was almost nauseated.

Then the facilitator said, *I know this has been heavy for you. I want you all to go outside and enjoy the gardens and breathe the fresh air and dance, wiggle, shiver—whatever you wish to do. Postulate that you are shaking off bad memories and any energy that you did not enjoy.*

I must say just being out there among the glorious flowers and little tinkling waterfalls, you just felt the lower vibes just lifting off of you. You see, now I realize I was healed in the Care Center so that that energy that permeated me from everyone telling her story really did not stick to me. We had to have that experience in order to process our Review, but then we could take a break and dance it off. It did not stay with us. It just disappeared because it no longer was a part of our life. We had looked at a very dreadful *movie* that was no longer part of our life.

After a little while, we were called back into the room. The room felt fresh and we were laughing and seemed to be at ease. We were assigned different places where we would be staying. I was kind of a loner and did not want to be in a house with a lot of people. We were given choices—kind of a dormitory, houses packed with people, or almost like a nice, small cottage with maybe a house mate or two. That is what I chose.

We were taken to our accommodations. When I saw my little house, I just loved it. It might have been small in stature, but inside it was quite spacious. Everything about it was perfect. I am still there and I just love it. My house mates and I are still healing, but we are compatible and we explore things together.

I can't think of anything else that I can talk about, unless you would like to ask me some questions.

Thank you for your story and yes, this is the time where I will ask you questions.

Questions (Q) and Answers (A)

Q: *My first questions is to clarify that you died at the age of 16?*

A: Yes, and after having my Review, I saw that I had chosen that life. I wanted to experience that on a soul level. Oh gosh, was that a hard choice. I only chose it for a couple of years. I'd rather die at 16 than die at 60, still a drug addict. Oh! So I did not have it for a long length of time as others had.

Q: *What have you been doing then in Heaven? You have been there quite a long time.*

A: Yes. I have been going to school. I have enjoyed that. I have been learning different things. I am very handy with my hands, and I have often been painting and learning about that. I think—it is just starting to gel in my mind—but I think when I return to Earth and have another lifetime, I will be a teacher. I will be an art teacher and teach the children to paint.

In painting, you can express your feelings, and it flows out of you onto the paper or canvas. It can be very healing; if I can get this idea across for the children, you see, they would have a medium, something they can use when they are really upset. If I had had that when I was an adult child…I'll put it that way. I could have been painting my frustrations with my family who I don't even remember. I could have been painting all of that. And maybe I would have had the sense to pick a different boyfriend or say no to him when he pushed his drugs at me.

It was like I did not have a moral fiber or something. By being an artist, I can put those dark emotions down on canvas. They can flow from me to something else. They are not eating me up. So that is what I want to do and that is what I have been doing.

Q: *Have you done any traveling?*

A: Oh yes. You know, when you have these artistic abilities or artistic calling, you travel because what you see you can put on canvas. I have seen so many beautiful areas I want to recapture. I am not into photography, so I did not want to replicate the scenes that way. I wanted to do it through my fingers and hands. As I worked more, I started getting more proficient so when I finished the picture, it actually looked like that place. I thought the paintings were quite good. Therefore, I traveled with my paints and found different places to paint.

Sometimes I would go to the ocean area. Other times I would go to a lake area, or to the mountains, or where there was snow, or the desert for the desert flowers. All of this was to feed this artistic ability that was germinating within me. Heaven has all of this. It is just exquisite. Anything you missed seeing while on Earth, you can see in Heaven. You could go to a Travel Log and if you had not seen it on Earth, you can see it in Heaven.

Maybe you wanted to see how the Chinese lived. There is an area that is somewhat Oriental. It has the beautiful Oriental buildings. They even have a kind of museum. You can go in and see the dress—what they wore in the different time periods. You can go to the Library and see even more. You can put on these CDs and hear their voices and get the translation. It is very interesting. It is not only China, but there are different cultural areas throughout Heaven.

Q: *Is there one particular area you are drawn to versus another?*

A: Not really; right now I am sort of in the exploring stage. But I imagine if I start being drawn to a particular area, it could be similar to where I will have my next Earth-body. I don't know. I am just starting to get that. Whether that is correct or not, I don't know. I am just starting to put that together.

Q: *Since you have been in Heaven, do you feel fulfilled?*

A: Not entirely. You see, I was only 16 when I died and I missed so much of life that I cannot say that I am fulfilled, for I did not live that long. I have so much catching up to do. I am still exploring. It is not a feeling of wanting to feel fulfilled, it is more a catching up on what I missed. I have to really work on not putting myself down—degrading myself. I have to keep reminding myself that it was my soul's choice, wanting that experience.

Q: *Do you feel that you have matured? Can you tell us about that process? You were just 16, so you have many years to gain wisdom and mature. Do you feel that you are doing that?*

A: Oh yes; I feel like I am probably around 30. That is always a nice number—a nice age. Of course, I have gained wisdom.

Q: *Do you still go to Group to speak to the facilitator to talk about something you want to know?*

A: I used to for a long time, but I do not any longer because I can ask my Angel who knows all about what I am asking.

Q: *Have you joined another group or is it just you and your housemates?*

A: I no longer have a body. I am in spirit form now. So I have a group with them that I have always had. They call it a *soul group*. I am with my soul group and they have become very close to me.

Q: *Are there just women in your soul group?*

A: Oh no, it is a co-ed group which is very fine because we get the man's perspective on things. You see, we go to the magnificent Library that is here in Heaven and we tune into what is going on in Earth. As a soul group, we discuss different options of what could be more productive and we watch the way the government in the United States struggles because the people who were voted in seem to come more from being anxious, trying to keep their position. They are into so much ego that nothing gets done, and the president struggles to try and maintain his pre-election promises which he finds is difficult to do. Therefore, we discuss things like that and we grow.

Q: *Do you have pets with you? Readers always like to know about this.*

A: Some do but I do not. You see, I was so on drugs in my Earth life that I did not have any money. You are not going to have money to feed a pet. You can adopt a stray dog or cat, but then you have to feed it. You barely have enough to feed yourself and still have money for your drugs. So you will not find too many people who are homeless and addicts having a pet they are taking care of also. So no, I wasn't into pets.

Q: *I am aware that the time here for this interview is almost over, but Sananda asks that I ask the subjects if you love yourself.*

A: Hmm, I am learning to; no, I did not love myself while on Earth, did I, when I was taking all of those drugs. I do not think any addict loves him or herself; it is impossible. I am just beginning to like myself, but no, I am not even sure how to answer or how that would look—to love myself

Q: *Is there a question you would like to ask me before we close this interview?*

A: No, I just admire the fact that you obviously have lived and are still going to live for many, many more years and have energy so clear and clean. I think to myself, *gosh, how did she do that?* (*Author chuckles.*) From this angle it is so clear and clean, and I say to myself, *gosh, I could have had that kind of energy if I had lived longer and had stopped being an addict.* But it was not my experience. I thank you for this opportunity—another experience that I had not realized was available to me. So I thank you.

And I and the readers thank you for sharing so honestly what that life was like and your death process. I admire your steadfastness, and I wish you well for your next life, for you know you will have one!

Yes, I can't get away from it, that's for sure.

I thank you again, and I wish you well and blessings to you.

Thank you!

All right, dear one, we have done it again. *Yes, my goodness sakes. (7:40 AM.) Thank you, Jeshua.* You are welcome, dear one. Talk to you later; love to you. *Thank you, Jeshua—over and out.*

8 CHIEF WOMAN

10-31-15 Chapter 8, 5:50 AM

You're starting early, dear one; I am Jeshua. Yes, I woke up and thought, why not just bring in Chapter 8? *All right sweetheart, we have a nice surprise for you as the next person comes forth. So I will step back and let her tell her story.* All right.

Oh my precious daughter, I am your mother. *Oh hi, Mom, how's it going?* That's what I am supposed to tell you, isn't it? We know we cannot say anything personal for the book, but we will speak afterwards, if that is all right. *Yes.*

It is interesting to know that I have the code name of CHIEF. And hello to this Author and all of the readers. The code name suits me quite well.

I grew up in a family who loved me very much, but it was so many years ago, in the pioneer days. I was born in 1892, so you see, many of the inventions had not been created yet.

I lived a long life. I was 94 when I died. However, my body was not in very good shape. I was totally deaf and totally blind—glaucoma. I regret hanging on so long, for at the end I was a burden to my daughter who had the sole responsibility of me. My other daughter lived in a different state and was too ill (MS) to come and share the care of me. My death was from a massive stroke. My daughter was visiting out of state at the time, but the housekeeper called my sister who lived about an hour away in another town. She came to me, as fast as her son could drive her here.

I just wanted out of my body. It was horrible. My sister called our doctor to come and then my daughter to question whether we ought to take me to the hospital for remedial care or to just let me pass. My daughter could not make the decision either and turned it back to my sister. It was finally agreed to let me go. My body was too far debilitated to try to resuscitate.

So actually, I slipped out of my body once everyone involved came to the sane conclusion to let me pass. I was surprised, for then my death was very easy—in that poor debilitated body one time and out of it the next moment. As the stories have been told from the other participants in this book, my Guardian Angel was there helping me also.

After a while, she asked me if I was ready to go on my journey. I knew I was going to Heaven. Therefore, I went to my sister and told her how much I loved her and thanked her. Of course she could not hear any of that. I went to my doctor and thanked him. He could not hear any of that either. I went to my housekeeper and thanked her. She also could not hear me. I went to my sister's son and thanked him for bringing his mother so promptly to me. Again there was no response. I thought to myself, *God, they are all as deaf as I am/was at this point (chuckles)*. I knew enough about metaphysics to know they could not see or hear me in the dimension I was now in.

My Angel then asked, *are you ready, my dear?* I said, *oh boy, am I. Let's go*. Then we more or less flew to Heaven, I'd guess you would say. I did go through the tunnel; it was quite an experience in itself. I kept my eyes open because I wanted to experience everything. I was surprised at how tired I was. Apparently, I was still carrying the lethargy from my death. When we arrived in Heaven, it was absolutely glorious, just glorious.

People wonder if your dead relatives will meet you. Yes, actually; there was my dear husband, my mother whom I loved very much, and various cousins, my brother. I saw them all. Everyone was greeting me and was so joyful. I was joyful also. If I were not so tired from my death, I would have had a great time. But my Angel said to me, *you can see all of them later on. We have to get you to the Care Center; you are still very weak. You have many things that need healing in that body, so let's go.* She just took my hand, and we went to the Care Center.

Of course, my room was lovely. It reminded me of my beautiful home—high ceiling, beautiful antique furniture—a blue room. She told me to undress and get into bed. I did and immediately fell asleep.

When I had my life, I requested that I wanted no funeral or memorial. It might have been old fashion thinking, but I did not want to put my friends through all of that. There were not that many left, actually. When you are 94, you do not have that many friends left (*chuckles*). I often kidded when I was alive, saying all of my bridge friends were dead so that when I died I could finally start playing bridge again—which I have, by the way.

Therefore, I had this long, healing sleep and did not have a dream where I visited my funeral to see the reactions of my family and friends. But I did have a dream where I did visit them. I went back to my old Victorian home. People were gathered. I visited my sister in her house in another town and visited my daughter who had her own house just a few miles away. I even went to see my daughter in another state who was so ill. They could not see or hear me, but I could hear them. They were all in their grief. It was a kind of broken up type of dream, and then I was just back in a dreamless asleep again.

My healing took many weeks, for there was so much wrong with my body. I could not hear and I could not see. Then the day that I woke up… Oh my goodness; I felt like I had been reborn. I had been reborn. I had this youthful body again. I had loved my body and here I was again in that body. They say you are always around 30, so I guess I was.

(I even wore some of the clothes I used to wear and loved.)

I woke up, threw back the covers, jumped out of bed. All of this I had not been able to do for so long. I could see; I could hear. Birds were singing outside. Of course, my Angel was there. I sort of just danced around the room. Oh… The amazing thing was I was highly educated in my Earth life—I was a professional woman trained in medicine, an MD. I had **retained** all of this. I had remembered it all very clearly. I could hardly wait to explore the scientific area in Heaven and see what they were doing along the medical line.

I was ravenous also. I was so hungry. All these things I had not been able to do for so long in my Earth body, for it was so debilitated. So my Angel said, *let's get you to the tea room so you can have a little bite there.* I said, *wonderful, for I am ravenous.* She took me to this sweet, little tea room. I had a wonderful cup of tea and a nice breakfast. I always remember that my mother made these marvelous, what we called, old-fashioned donuts. And there they were, those same kinds of donuts! I always loved a soft boiled egg also and there it was, a soft boiled egg. This time I could see them all because with my blindness, I had not seen all of this for so long. Oh, I enjoyed that breakfast.

Then came the hard part. My Angel said to me, *you know what is coming next.* I said, *yeah, I've got to go to the Review room for hours and watch my past life.* And this I did. There were periods of my life that were very difficult. I sat in front of this big screen and watched it all play out. I don't think whoever puts that on missed a beat.

I saw where I was with my little 5 year old daughter at the hospital and she was battling diphtheria for her life. I was with her day and night for she almost slipped away. I mentally kept calling her back until she came to from the coma she was in. She doesn't remember a thing about it. But we got her back to the little house on the prune ranch we were renting. I saw my husband, her Daddy, bring her an ice cream cone every afternoon. Our house was quarantined so he had to climb a ladder to her window in order to see her. He had been staying at a neighbor's so he could continue his orthodontia practice and not become ill. No one else got the disease in our household.

It was a pleasure to see our daughter literally come back to life. We loved her so much. Then we bought this old Victorian 14 room mansion. This became my life, my passion, in decorating it. I looked forward to bringing it to its former glory, a project that took many devoted years.

So I sat at the Review screen and saw all of that; experienced the death of my husband, mother, and other relatives, too numerous to list now. And then it was finished. Strangely enough I was so healed and so well by now that after it was over, it was a great release, for it had ended that lifetime. It brought it to closure for me. I think that is one of the reasons for the Review. It brings your past life to closure. Then you could just let it all go. Since I was so healthy now, it was like the end of a bad movie, although there were good parts. But I could just let it all go! I felt lighter.

I then jumped up and exclaimed, *OK, that's done! What's next?* My Angel said, *now we are going to go to a group of many, many people who died around the same time you did.* Therefore, we went to this room this Author calls the *Group Processing* room, and it was, actually. We all told our story. I was one of the oldest ones there. It is kind of interesting because everyone had been healed and when someone would ask me how old I was and I said 94, they would all look at me incredulously. I looked like I was 30 as I am jumping around at 94.

People would exclaimed, *but that is incredible; look at you*! And I'd say, *yes, look at me*! The marvelous part of it was I had retained all of my education and profession, and I could hardly wait to explore. As a pioneer doctor, I wanted to see and hear what was new in the medical field—what is new now!

You see, when I was getting so blind, I had to retire when I was about 75. There is a big gap in there. I wanted to know if they had found a cure for Multiple Sclerosis (MS), since my daughter had had that—not the one who was with me but her sister who lived in another state. I was hoping they would have that cure by now. Sadly, they do not.

I also found out that these different diseases kind of have their own timing. I remember when polio was sweeping the nation and so many people were getting it, like President Roosevelt. Then they came up with the serum—the Salk's' vaccine. Thereby, no one had to have polio anymore. I thought to myself, *it must not be the right timing for MS*. So many people have MS, and I know the soul chooses that for different reasons. Maybe that is why the cure has not been found, because the timing is not ready for it. Souls need these different illnesses and experiences in order to grow. I think it is about time that dreaded disease is eradicated. It is every bit as horrible as the polio was. I believe it is time MS is taken from Earth!

To get back to the processing room, it was very interesting to hear about the various deaths and the age groups. I understood I might have been the oldest, and there were those who were a lot younger than I. However, for a soul comprehension and level, we were all fairly comparable.

So we heard everybody's stories. The facilitator was there. Then when we were being assigned our accommodations, I joyfully was able to join my mother where she lived. Isn't that wonderful? You not only get to see them but you can go live with them. The others in that group were assigned to a dormitory or house or whatever, but here I am, able to just go and live with my mother again. Of course, we are on equal terms, but when you love that person, it is wonderful to just go and be with her. So that is what I did.

She has a lovely house and of course—you know, you can create anything you want in Heaven. My mother was an old pioneer and loved some of the Earth places she had stayed. So she had a farm house which was kind of pleasing. Then of course when I came to live with her—you can make these changes—and I said *Mom why don't we do this?* And before you'd know it, I was redecorating her house (*chuckles*). She did not care.

Then I met other relatives. I could tell who was in my soul group and who was not. Those who were in my soul group I immediately had a bonding with. The other relatives I just had a brief connection with. I did not think of them that much. The connection was on Earth.

You see, when you are up in Heaven and relatives are not of your soul group, after a while it is almost like the kids at school in your class room. You know them but you don't spend time with all of them or are close to them. That is how it is here. When you see relatives who are not of your soul group, you really do not spend that much time with them anymore.

Now let's see. Oh, I know. I was talking with my mother, and she was telling me about the different areas in Heaven. She said, *have your Angel take you to where all of the medical creation is happening— wonderful things are being created.* So I more or less have been hanging out there.

I have not decided whether to reincarnate or just work at a spiritual level here. I have a choice, you see. I can go back to Earth and have another life. But I had reached the pinnacle of that lifetime, actually. Until Earth has some healings of its own, I would not be able to do that much for it, for the people. I could do more for them while I am in Heaven. So I have not gone back.

I could even go to another planet, other Universes, but I don't think I will. I am just enjoying being with my soul group. And yes, I have dropped that body now and am in spirit form. I no longer want to eat, particularly. My soul group is very large. There are different areas where I am exploring and still studying. I have been in the medical field for so long. However, I have enjoyed the arts, the music. So I was taking piano lessons before I dropped my body. A group of us have similar talents and interests, shall we say. We kind of explore Heaven in a group.

My group is more scientifically minded, so we spend a great deal of time in the laboratories and teaching halls. I teach the younger souls. I help souls who will become doctors while on Earth. While my methods may have been old fashioned, there are still things I can teach them.

Woman doctors are more respected on Earth now than they were when I was one. As I look back, it was ridiculous, for a woman doctor was treated as if she were in the nurse category. The men all wore suits and the women doctors were in nurses' uniforms, so to speak. It was an interesting life, rising above that prejudice.

I can't think of anything more that I can tell you. I have read the book—a very interesting book—while I am in Heaven. So I guess I will just turn this back over to you, Author, for the Question and Answer period.

Yes, thank you, for that will be what we discuss next.

Questions (Q) and Answers (A)

Q: *I am not quite sure as to what questions to ask you. Lord Sananda always likes me to ask,* do you love yourself?

A: Oh I do! On Earth, that was the problem. I loved my body so much that I would not leave it! I could not see nor hear, and yet I just did not want to leave that body! Of course, that has gotten me into trouble. Here in Heaven I love myself in the spirit form. So yes, I do love myself.

Q: *Have you seen any of the Ascended Masters?*

A: Yes, I have. I have seen our Lord Jesus/Sananda. His Light is so brilliant that it always astonishes me. So yes, I have met with him. We are quite close, actually. We talk about philosophy and the future of medicine and the aspects that will be discovered and healed. I am very excited about it. When he came to me to ask if I would agree to be a subject for this book, of course I jumped at it.

Q: *Is there anything that you deeply regret that you did not do when you had your Earth life?*

A: Yes, I in some ways… I was so dedicated to my profession, and I loved my family dearly, but in some ways I was not tuned into my family as I could have been. There were things with my daughter I was not on top of. I still had that kind of pioneer mentality. Take clothes, for example. We did not change into a new outfit every day. You wore something and you wore it for a week. I did not realize when my daughter was in high school, children no longer did that. They wore something different every day. So I did not see the pain she was going through because her wardrobe was not that extensive. She had to wear the same outfit repeatedly. The other children were making fun of her, bringing her to tears.

I looked back on that and thought, *oh, my gosh, how could I have been so unconscious of the fact that young girls need more outfits?* I could have afforded that. It was not the lack of money. It just was not in my mind-set. For me, one outfit per week would do it. However, that does not fly in high school, does it? So I feel sad about that. That's my regret.

Q: *While you are in Heaven, do you feel fulfilled? Do you feel that you have a reason to be, shall we say?*

A: Yes, I do. I am fulfilled. I still love the medical, educated part of me—the scientific part of me. And I have been delving into the artistic part also. I love decorating, fabrics, and sewing. I could do all of that; so I have enjoyed doing that again. Even though you are in spirit body, you can do all of this. So I have done so.

Q: *I am aware that I am running out of time here and that this interview must end. So I will ask you, as I have asked all of the subjects, do you have a question for me?*

A: Oh, dear Author, I do not have a question, but I would like to make a comment that what you are doing is in the category for me, unbelievable! And I thank you for giving me the privilege of being one of your subjects.

Q: *You are most welcome. I thank you also and am honored that you have come. So with that, we will end this interview for this book. I give you my blessings.*

A: Thank you, dear Author, thank you.

Well, dear one that was Chapter 8. *Yes, thank you, Jeshua.* You are welcome, dear one; love to you.

Thank you, love to you, too. 6:45 AM.

9 CLERGY WOMAN

1 1-08-2015 Sunday 7:20 AM.

All right, precious one, bright and early to start our next chapter, Chapter 9. This next Being is all ready to step forth as I step back. *All right, thank you.*

Good morning, dear Author; I am your next subject, and I understand I am to tell you about my death and entrance into Heaven.

Good morning to you, and yes, that is correct. Thank you for coming.

My death was not particularly dramatic compared to many of the others, but of course, when it happens to you, it is dramatic to you.

I was in an automobile accident. I did not have my seatbelt fastened. I was in the back seat with other members of my family. While my mother and father in the front seat had their belts on, we in the back had not bothered. My father was a careful driver, but this obviously was meant to be, for we were *T-boned*—the expression that is used when a car crashes midsection into another car. The car that crashed into us was not a dinky one. I don't know cars; I just know it was large. It might be called an SUV.

No one else was killed or had to go to the hospital. So obviously, it was my time to go. I remember sitting in my seat and everybody was talking at once when all of a sudden, WHAM, and I was thrown out.

How one can get ejected out of a car is hard to imagine. But I just got propelled out of the car.

I really did not feel any pain particularly, but one minute I am in my body and the next minute I am standing outside of it—all in a daze trying to figure out what's going on. This woman who I now know is my Guardian Angel held my hand because now that I was out of my body, I was just very confused. I probably would have just started running off into on-coming traffic. But it would not have made any difference, for I was in a different dimension. (You can't kill me twice!)

She slowed me down a bit and said, *dear one, dear one, you have been in a terrible car accident and your body has been killed. That is why you feel so confused.* She said, *let's leave this scene. We no longer need to be here. The police have come and are taking care of everything. They will take your body to wherever your parents want you to go.* You see, they did not have to identify the body because everyone could tell them who I was.

I held her hand and off we went. I did go through the tunnel. It was a sunny day, but it got kind of twilight again. My Angel could still talk to me. We could still communicate going a thousand miles per hour or whatever the speed was through this tunnel. It was kind of dim in there, and I asked for explanations. She said, *you are in the tunnel that is taking you to Heaven. Just relax; I will take care of you. There is nothing to worry about. I will not lose my grip on you and you are safe.*

Then to give my mind something else to think about, she started asking me things about my life. She knew all the answers, but she wanted me to think of happy times; *what was your happiest memory?* She asked me other questions. As I look back on this, it seems strange that we were carrying on this conversation and whooshing to Heaven at the same time—like an airplane; I guess.

Sure enough, we arrived. For me, it was absolutely amazing. It is so much more than I had ever realized or known. Heaven can overwhelm you when you first come. Heaven is so huge and so beautiful, so Light. The gardens are absolutely amazing.

So we came to this gentle landing. My Angel just let me stand for a few minutes to let me pivot around in order to take it all in and get a little bit oriented. She took my hand again and told me we were going to the Care Center, as I needed to be healed. *The car crash hurt your body quite severely. You have many internal injuries.* I just thought it was kind of peculiar how I could be injured inside from the crash. I guess it was from the impact.

She took me to the Care Center. I had a pretty little room. It was in shades of pink with roses on the wallpaper. It was very inviting. I was feeling very sleepy. She said to me to take my clothes off and get into bed, which I did. I can barely remember what I did, as I was half asleep as I crawled into bed. She was helping me put the covers over me. I was gone; I was fast asleep.

Apparently, I was asleep for several weeks. During that time, I had a dream where I went to my funeral and there were a lot of my classmates there. Everybody was crying. It was kind of interesting to me, for so many of my class- mates from school had come, even people I did not think liked me very well. They were there looking kind of somber and saying, *I did not know her very well, but I just wanted to come so she would know that I had come.*

Then, of course, my mother and father and the rest the family came—my brother and a couple of sisters, aunts and uncles, neighbors. Everybody was there. I had this little dog and they even brought my dog—Sparky. He saw me and was jumping around and barking. And they kept saying, *hush, Sparky, hush.* They did not get why he was barking while he was joyfully greeting me. I could actually pet him. I murmured to him, *stop barking now; it is all right.* Then he sort of settled down.

I did not stay all that long. You know when you are in the flesh and go to something like that on the human side, you are interested to see what food would be served. There was a nice luncheon after the services. I always liked eating, so I was kind of disturbed that I could not eat any of it. There was Jell-O. I loved Jell-O.

Then my Angel said, *all right, dear one; it is time to go back.* The next thing I knew, I was back in bed and sound asleep again! I don't think I had ever left my bed. I don't understand how that works. I slept some more.

Then one day I just woke up. I was healed. It was a wonderful feeling. I was in better shape then than I was before the car accident. There was a green robe at the foot of my bed. My Angel said to put that on, which I did.

She asked if I wanted anything to eat. I replied that I was thirsty so she took me to this place—I don't know if it was a tea room or a café. People were having kind of muted conversations. You could not hear what anyone else was saying. It seemed as if everyone was whispering. I could not understand why the talking was so muted. But that might have just been my perception.

I had some hot chocolate and a wonderful muffin. There was some fresh fruit, but I was not drawn to eat that. After a while, my Angel said it was time for me to go to the Review Room. It dawned on me. *Oh yes, I had to sit in front of a screen and watch my life from start to finish. What a joy that will be—NOT.* But it was all part of the process, so it was best to just get it over with.

Actually, it was not as bad as I thought it might be. I saw where I could have been more compassionate, more loving with members of my family, but I was just a teenager—just starting my high school years—sweet 16. I was looking forward to my 16th birthday. So be it; it was not in my cards. I did not need to stay that long in the Review Room. Some people were there for hours. I guess it all depends on how old you were when you died, as to how long a Review you were going to have. I was 15. You can zip through many years on a screen at 15, going on 16.

So that was done. I then asked my Angel, *OK, what's next?* She took me to the Group Processing Room where everybody talks about her death. I did not realize that we would be discussing all the different deaths and explanations of what has gone on. We went into this group room and there were maybe about 50 of us there. You put 50 people in a large room, and it does not seem like that many.

The facilitator came in and she had each of us tell about our death. I guess that was to make sure that the person would know that she had died. It had not occurred to me that people can die and not know it. Everybody in my group knew we were dead. Death is always a shock because you do not expect it—alive one minute and dead the next. It is an adjustment. It is such an adjustment.

Then the facilitator said that we could now pick our accommodations as to where we wanted to live. I noticed that some people were not going to be there very long. They were going to go right back to a new Earth life. So the facilitator assigned them into a dormitory, and everyone knew she was going to go right back but no one knew why. We tried not to invade their privacy by asking, *how come you are going back so soon?* Others could not wait to go back, so that was a whole other processing that they did. We were kind of divided up, actually. Those who were going to go right back were put into one group and taken to another partition of the room. We could not hear what they were saying and vice versa.

It is very interesting how in Heaven—and I don't know how that is done—but they can compartmentalize the sound in some way. You can hear very clearly where you are, but just a few steps away you could not hear the other person at all, if that was the way it was going to be set up. When I was in the Review Room, I heard nothing that was outside of my perimeter. It was the same way in this processing room.

There was the group that was to go back immediately and you could not hear why. They had their own facilitator. It was puzzling to me.

But to get back to me, I did not know anybody, but there were several age groups. Later I learned what level you were at in your soul development played…If you were only 10 and your soul development was high, you could be with people who were older than you. How can I put this? Like the body age made no difference. It was the soul age that guided where you would—who you would be hooked up with, so to speak. While there were different body ages in that processing group, it was the ages of the soul evolution that was counted. That soul level…We were all kind of on the same page then. And it was hard to break from that Earth mentality, mind-set, because you were used to looking at a 10-year-old and not expecting the person to know what you know. But her soul and your soul were on the same page—kind of a mind-set that we worked with in those groups.

We could wait to be assigned with someone else or we could just say our preference—live in a dormitory-type life or a small home. No one was without a housemate. Everyone had to have at least one other person with her. That could change after you had been in Heaven for a while, but in the beginning we were paired off.

I was paired off with another—since I was in that mind set of a school girl—I was paired off with another girl, we'll say (*versus a woman*). There is this buddy system and the two of us chose a place where we would be with a few other people. We did not want a dormitory, per se. Therefore, we chose a small house with a few other people, but not a whole bunch.

We were taken there and it was a very nice house. It had its own kitchen and there were no house rules. You could do just what you wanted to do but you did it in pairs—the buddy system for now. Of course, after you have lived in Heaven for a while, you can change where you want to live—relatives and so forth.

I do not know what else to say, particularly. I know there is a Question and Answer segment. So, Author, do you want me to say anything else?

Thank you for your story for me and the readers. And yes, we will continue with the Question and Answer period.

Questions (Q) and Answers (A)

Q: *You mentioned your pet, Sparky. Has he joined you yet or is he still alive?*

A: Oh, my dear Sparky. He is with me now. I have been in Heaven for a number of years; the presidents in America have come and gone, so I have my dear Sparky with me.

Q: *Who was president while you were on Earth?*

A: Oh, it was President Kennedy (*Jan.20, 1961 – Nov. 22, 1963.*) Everybody loved him, and when he was assassinated, there was such a pouring out of grief. He was greatly missed when I was alive.

Q: *The readers always like to know what the people have been doing while in Heaven. Since you have been there quite a while, what have you been doing with your time?*

A: Well, my housemate, my buddy, and I have traveled a great deal. The wonderful thing is, when we finally realized it, you cannot get lost. Nobody can get lost in Heaven! It is sort of amazing. While I was on Earth, I never thought about going anywhere by myself, for my parents would always take me. But in Heaven, you always have your Angel. I wanted to see some waterfalls. So I asked my Angel how we could find some waterfalls. She suggested we might like to take an airplane trip to the falls. That astounded me. I did not know they had airplanes in Heaven. (*Readers: in the previous book, Military Man tells of his passion with airplanes and how he flies frequently with his Angel by his side.*)

Therefore, my buddy and I did fly and have gone on boat rides, trains, and buses. We have tried it all. It is fantastic. And yes, there are falls all over the place—beautiful. The scenery is just gorgeous.

On Earth, if something is going to be extra good, it is called 5 Star. Well I am telling you Heaven is way above a 5 Star—more a 10 Star! When one first leaves Earth, it is just astounding because everything is so much more. Even a flower is more beautiful; an animal is more beautiful.

We go to where the animal energy area is; it is hard to explain, but it is like a petting zoo! The whole thing is open. There are no cages, no fences. The whole thing is a petting zoo. We would go to just to try it out. We wanted to see some baby tigers and so forth. For some reason, we would just be there. There would be these mothers with their baby cubs. We could just walk up to them.

We would squat down and the mothers would let you take their baby cub and just hold it—just like a kitten on Earth. You could just nuzzle that precious little animal. The mother would just be glowing with pride, for she could feel your love for her baby. It was wonderful. You could scratch her behind her ears, and she would purr and lick you. You would not dare to be licked on Earth. You would be eaten, but the animals do not eat meat here. It was just so much fun being with the animals with no fear between either of us. So my buddy and I have spent a lot of time there. That is where Sparky was when he first passed. He went to Animal Heaven, we call it.

Q: *What form are you in now—still in the body or now in spirit form?*

A: I am in my spirit form now. I had dropped my body quite a while ago. It is interesting, because you are not mentally thinking to yourself, *tomorrow I am going to drop my body and just be in spirit form.* It does not happen like that. It is—oh gosh…It sneaks up on you; let's put it that way. (*Subject struggles with how to describe the process.*)

You get to the point where you are no longer eating. You are not hungry, and it does not register mentally that you have missed a meal. Time is different here. You get involved with something, and then you realize that you had not eaten for that day. Then that could go on for 2-3 days.

Everything is an adjustment because you are changing your mind-set until it registers that you are no longer eating or need to. You still have the facilitator you can go to in Group Process if you are confused and need some counseling. There is an energy in that room that seems to resolve one's concerns. You leave there feeling calm and no longer do you feel there is/was a problem. (Wish that was available on Earth. There are a lot of teenagers who could use that energy.)

Q: *What about relationships? How are they chosen for when you reincarnate. Have you met him or her?*

A: I have met the people who will be my family. We have had long discussions that are unique to each of us—who is going to be my father and mother and why. We go to the Records and can see what we still have to resolve with that person. It is very complicated. You are... You have this companion and he or she guides you through all of this. I guess the person is from your soul group so that your life is mapped out as to whom you are going to meet.

It is interesting because I never had a real boyfriend on Earth. I was only fifteen (*going on 16*), so I was still fairly naïve. Not having a boyfriend, I did not get into the whole sex game. So here I am up in Heaven and everyone in my soul group is gathered. It is like a class—a class on sexuality. They are teaching about sex between a man and a woman, or two women, or two men. They go into it all on homosexuality. Now when you get to Earth, you will know about all of this.

It is ridiculous that there is such controversy about all of the different aspects of sexuality. But when you get to Earth, the veil or amnesia comes upon you so that you do not remember the teachings you got in Heaven. If you join a church on Earth and that church is so against same-sex couples marrying, then there is this huge controversy if that rule is broken. And yet Heaven is teaching that there are souls who want that experience. There is so much to learn when your partner is of the same sex. That is not allowed on Earth. Therefore, we get into all of that as we plan our next lifetime.

I don't remember what you had asked me that led into all of that on sexuality (*chuckles*).

I don't either (smiles), but it was very informative and interesting!

Q: *Time-wise we are coming to the end of this interview. You talked of your soul group after you had dropped your body.*

A: Yes; after you drop your body, you meet up with your soul group. There are different ones you gravitate to and he or she becomes your teacher. When I died, I was a female, but in my soul group you are androgynous. You can go to a soul where the energy is more masculine. So you can have a soul who carries both masculine and feminine energies but prefers the dominance of the one over the other. (*Author: I have a more masculine soul; Jesus has chosen a more feminine soul. Rarely are we balanced when in an Earth body.*)

Q: *When you reincarnate, you will be with the families and teachers that you had set up in Heaven. Is that what you were telling me?*

A: Yes, that was what I was meaning when I got off track with the sexuality topic.

Q: *Sananda wants me to ask if you love yourself.*

A: Yes, I do; I always have, even when I had my Earth life, I loved myself. In my soul group, we of course are all operating on the level of unconditional love and it is quite wonderful. That is another thing—when you reincarnate and you pick your family, not everyone will carry unconditional love. That is why you can have a sibling who may be jealous of you; or a spouse whose love is more possessive. These are the lessons your soul has set up for you—that was part of your contract to be played out, so it could learn.

Q: *We have come to the end of this interview. Is there anything you would like to ask me or comment on?*

A: Oh, I have not thought of that, but thank you for asking. I just want to make a comment that I thoroughly enjoyed this. I read your first book and liked it so much. I look forward to reading this one and the other subjects' stories also. So I thank you.

Q: *And I thank you for being so gracious and so honest with the telling of your story. I have enjoyed talking to you, and I wish you all the best and ask God to bless you mightily in your next Earth journey.*

A: Thank you very, very much, dear Author.

You are most welcome. Bye for now. Bye.

All right, dear one; you did it again.

Oh my goodness, she brought in a lot of different information; I am sure the readers will enjoy that.

Yes; this is it for now, dear one…until Chapter 10.

Yes, thank you, Jeshua; Namaste.

Namaste to you too, precious one.

8:20 AM.

10 MILITARY WOMAN

1 1-19-2015 Thursday 7:00 AM.

Hello, precious one, you are all set to go with our final chapter of the different subjects; then later on we will bring an Ascended Master for the closing chapter. *Yes.* All right, our last subject is ready to tell her story.

Oh, dear Author, I am so excited. I have never done this before—oh, golly, I don't quite know what to expect, although I did read the previous book. I have some idea, I guess, but I am waiting for you to say something.

Hello, dear one, I am so thankful for your coming. And yes, this is where you get to tell your story. I will then ask questions.

All right. My death was quite awful. It was by asphyxiation. I couldn't breathe; I just couldn't breathe. I had some type of illness (*Chronic Obstructive Pulmonary Disease*; *C.O.P.D.*). I awoke in the middle of the night and I was by myself, fighting to catch a breath. I simply could not breathe. I was not near a telephone; I could not get out of bed. Then I just fainted and never woke up in my body again. I guess it was my time, but oh, it was dreadful, just dreadful—the thrashing, trying to gulp for air that was not there.

The next thing I knew was my Guardian Angel (which I found out later was the woman with me) had her arms around me and I said, not knowing I had died, *oh gosh, what took you so long? I couldn't breathe and I was crying for someone to come. What took you so long?* She said, *dear one, I was always here; I had not left your side. You could not breathe and you passed from your body. You died and you are now in my arms, and I am protecting you. It is finished.*

I excitedly retorted, *what do you mean it is finished? What's finished?* She said, *your life, dear one. This was your time to pass from your body, and you have done that. Your death process was what your soul wanted to experience.* I was screaming and exclaimed, *well, I guess I won't do that again!*

My Angel just squeezed my hand and said, *no, not unless you write that up in your contract again.* Of course, that raised all sorts of questions, but at that time I did not feel like asking more questions. I was between two worlds, and it took too much effort to figure it all out. I was not what one would call a *happy camper.* I was disgruntled and mixed up and just hung on to my Angel for dear life.

My Angel said, *come along, dear one, we will now journey to Heaven.* Every time she said something, it just brought up all of this strangeness and all of these questions I was afraid to ask. So I did not say anything. I was totally confused and just turned myself over to her hands. All the time she kept talking and murmuring to me, I did not know that we were traveling at the speed of Light! She had her arms around me and was cradling my head against her shoulder. I kept my eyes closed. I did not know that we had moved! The whole thing was very weird. But I just gave myself over to her. She kept murmuring, *hush, dear one; hush. All is right; all is fine.*

The next thing I knew was when she said, *all right, dear one, we are here.* I was not sure what she was talking about, so I said, *where is here?* I lifted my head off her shoulder and she said, *why, Heaven, dear one; we have flown to Heaven.* Of course, by that time I was so astounded that I couldn't talk. I just stared around bug-eyed at this gorgeous place, still trying to figure it all out with my mouth hanging open, I guess (*chuckles*), and with my eyes bugged out. Oh, my gosh…

My Angel said to me, *come, dear one, you will calm down soon. I am taking you to the Care Center and you will have a nice rest. And when you wake up you will be totally oriented and all will be explained to you.* By that time I was feeling very tired. I guess anybody who had traveled this far would be tired too (*chuckles*), but I did not know that.

Therefore, we went to the Care Center and to this very pleasing room—colors that I liked in blues, lavenders in kind of stripes or something. She told me to take my gown off. I was surprised that I still had that on. How could I have traveled all those miles in my night gown? You know, by that time you are so confused, at least I was, that you just give up on trying to figure it all out. So I took my gown off and crawled into bed. I was out like a light.

Then I had the dream—like the others I had talked to—of my funeral, seeing my family. I was not married but had a boyfriend. He was there looking kind of astounded. No one could believe I had passed. They were all wondering how this could have happened. I guess there is a name for it now, C.O.P.D. Oh, I don't want to talk about it. It's *over and done with* as the saying goes. So I did the whole funeral thing; people were there. Some were crying. Others were just walking around in a daze. They were as shocked as I was, I guess.

It was interesting, too, for me because I could pick out those people who were there who would not live much longer themselves! It was sort of like I just knew it. There was a teacher there from my high school and I just knew he had not much longer to live himself! So I just kind of made note of those observations. The next thing I knew, I was back, dreaming away.

Apparently I slept for several weeks and was being healed all that time. I had no memory of what they did with me. There was a lot of Light; I remember that part. There were also soothing sounds. You are so sleepy that you cannot stay awake, but the next thing I knew, I was awake.

I sat up; threw the covers back and hopped out of bed like I did when I was in a nice, healthy body. I felt wonderful. I was joyous. I noticed that my hands were also healed, for I had had some warts on them and they were all healed too. I thought, *that's interesting!*

My Angel was there right on cue. She said, *well, dear one, you are looking chirper.* I replied, *yes, I feel wonderful.* She asked me if I would like a bite to eat. I said, *oh yes, I could eat a huge breakfast.* So we went to the tea room or whatever it is called. I had a cup of tea, some scrambled eggs, and one of those nice muffins and some delicious melon.

After I ate I wanted to brush my teeth. She told me there was a restroom over there where I could brush my teeth off. I went into the restroom and over the sink were packets of a toothbrush and toothpaste. I brushed my teeth and rinsed my mouth. There were paper cups—gosh, how do I explain this—they were like paper cups, but they weren't because they were clear. There was a basket near the sink, and you put your disposed articles in the basket. You just tossed your stuff in, but it kept going—just disappeared. It was like a basket that did not have a bottom! It was very strange.

I looked in the mirror and noticed how clear my complexion was. I looked great. I was delighted. I spread my lips to look at my teeth and they were just perfect. I always had had a tooth that was kind of protruding. Even that was straight. Goodness sake; they even straighten your teeth! I thought that was miraculous.

Then she took me to the Review room. I sat and watched my short life. I say *short life* compared to all the others, I guess. You know when you have your life you had done some stuff you were not too proud of. Now you had to see it all again and feel all of it again. But on the whole; it was more going down *Memory Lane* than anything. I was what you would call a *good kid* and had not gotten into too much trouble.

After that we went either to another room or building. It probably was another building because where you have your Review is huge. It is kind of weird up here in Heaven, because when you think of something, you are just there. So when she said we were going to another place to meet another group, we were just there! And it is difficult to ascertain whether your new spot is in another room or building. However, it was a large room with a lot of people all milling around in what was called the *Group Processing* room, I found out.

The facilitator came in and had us tell our stories. There were others who had died as I had. But their asphyxiation was in different ways. One was murdered with a pillow put over her head, and stuff like that. We heard it all—some had died in childbirth.

After that we were assigned places where we were going to stay. I still had that kind of mentality of being on a trip and having to find a place to stay. I did not think of it as being my permanent home for the next whatever years. I was thinking like a teenager; so I chose a dormitory. I had noticed that in the Processing room there were different age groups. But it was soul awareness that had grouped us together like this. There were a bunch of people who were teenagers, so we were assigned to this dormitory place per our requests.

We had nice individual rooms, but there was a common hall and a common kitchen—you know, a regular dormitory. By the time we went off to our different places to stay, we knew the people from the Group Processing room pretty well. You quickly get a buddy system going. Later I found out you kind of gravitate to those who are in your soul group. There were others who were not of the same soul group, so the two groups kind of buddied within each other.

Therefore, we went to this nice dormitory. That is about all I can say about my entrance into Heaven. So I will turn it back to you, Author, and let you have your questions.

All right, thank you so much. It is always interesting for me and the readers to hear/read the different stories about the various entrances into Heaven. Now we will have the question-and-answer phase of this interview.

Questions (Q) and Answers (A)

Q: *Let's establish the age that you died so we can kind of figure out how long you have been in Heaven.*

A: Yes, I was…I can't quite remember my age when I died—17 or 18, something like that. I just know…Oh, I remember. It was around the same time that our President died—President Franklin Delano Roosevelt, FDR (*April 12, 1945*). I had not graduated from high school yet but was getting ready for college.

Q: *So tell us what you have been doing. Have you been assigned to any particular job? How does that work?*

A: Well, after we had lived in our accommodations and had kind of settled in…You have a time period where you can explore, for there is so much to see. You can go to the library, museums, and again, you do not have to worry about how you are going to get there. Nobody can get lost. You have your Angel with you all the time. She kind of guides you. You go to different areas in Heaven that you have not experienced before when you had your Earth lifetime. But you had been there in past lives.

I remembered I loved Thailand and loved the way they bent their fingers when they danced. So I wanted to see Thailand. There was a group of us from our dormitory and then we were just there in Thailand, so to speak. There are areas all over Heaven that have different cultures. If you were a "Thailand-ese," you would feel right at home there in that area because that is what is familiar and known to you. They have the canals and the boats that people maneuvered around by a pole. It was fascinating to me.

But to get back to your question, I was supposed to teach if I had lived long enough. Then it gets back to the question, *what are you going to teach?* As I traveled around—I am smiling now—I was very interested in the culinary arts. I was going to teach people how to cook different things. There is a bakery chef here, and I have enjoyed baking all of these wonderful, delicious desserts.

Therefore, to answer your question, I was not particularly assigned, but I was asked if I could help out here. They always make it sound like it is your idea—*would you really like to come and help out*—instead of saying, *you are assigned to this.* Of course, I jumped at the chance. I learned a great deal—stuff that I had not known before about cooking and baking. So that is what I have been doing.

Q: *When you have your next Earth life, is it too soon to say Master Chef?*

A: I don't know; maybe. I have been here a long time, that's for sure. I know I will have to go back. I have been meeting with my soul group, and we are putting together my next life. We haven't quite completed the preliminaries yet. There is so much to think about when you get together to arrange your next lifetime.

You have to pick everyone you will be meeting. I even have talked to who would be my teacher in that next lifetime, and I would be studying under him—a male cook. I have had all that training up in Heaven before I even incarnate. I find that fascinating.

Q: *You have been in Heaven a long time and are getting ready to reincarnate, it sounds like. That veil of forgetfulness—amnesia—will come over you when you get to Earth, but if someone were to ask you what would you say was your most significant experience while in Heaven, what would you answer?*

A: I think the fact that—how can I put this—it has to do with the energy of Heaven. It is multidimensional, and it has all of these aspects. There is so much love and you feel the peace, so you are very calm. You could be excited about something, but you do not get hysterical like you could on Earth. This love just emanates from everything. You could go up to a live tree and put your arms around its trunk and you will feel its love! Or you can go to the animal section and all of the animals are loving you as you are loving them. It is just astounding—peace and love—it is just astounding.

Q: *Speaking of the animal section and the pets, are you introduced to the pet you will have on Earth?*

A: Not per se; there can be pets that you have had in a previous lifetime who can carry over to the next lifetime. Therefore, you would meet those; but if you had a pet and it died or you died, there still is a choice as to whether you would not have any pets; or you could have a different one in the next lifetime. Say you had a cat in the previous lifetime and this time around you have a dog, or vice versa. So that can change.

However, there are people who are getting ready to reincarnate, and they spend a lot of time with their pet that they are going to have again on Earth. There are a lot of people who have a great love for horses; so this can be carried forth from lifetime to lifetime. It is almost like that pet energy can be reincarnated also, but it is not quite as it sounds and I do not understand it enough to explain it to you. However, when you again have an Earth body, you can have a pet that you had had in another lifetime.

Q: *You have met your soul group by this time and you are now in spirit form. Is this correct?*

A: Yes, I stopped the eating, but I can still enjoy what I have cooked if I wish to. But I am with my soul group. And I did not realize it, but a soul group has different dimensions to it. It is always evolving. That is when you get to be with the Ascended Masters, because you have now reached that level. However, you still are not quite able to catch up with them. Some of the souls become Masters but most have to develop more. It is with the help of these higher Beings in your soul group who have nudged you that it is time to return to Earth in order to grow more. You can learn just so much in Heaven, but it is the actual physical part of doing something that brings you the wisdom, you see. So there is a great deal ahead of me still that I need to experience, which becomes the knowledge which becomes the wisdom which you can now carry forth into each lifetime.

Q: *I am aware of our time with the interview drawing to a close. I ask each of the subjects if there is anything you would like to ask me.*

A: I am just curious. As you telepathically interview people and put the answers in a book, can anyone do that? Do you have to be kind of assigned to do that? I also see where you are highly educated with a doctorate. Again, can anyone do that?

Q: *Those are interesting questions. Yes, I will say that anyone can do what I have done. You train your telepathic abilities. Then as you connect with a Master, he or she becomes your gatekeeper. You set it up to interview people. If you wish the information to be in book form, you learn how to put a book together and send it off to a publishing firm.*

As far as a Ph.D., YES. Anyone who wishes to study for many years and create a research project can do that. (I devoted 10 years to my doctorate goal.) It just takes a lot of dedication, discipline. But keep in mind, while anyone can do what I have done, what is the purpose for doing this? Maybe it is not that person's purpose to spend that much time in pursuit of a doctorate. Again, so much of it depends on what your contracts are. Maybe you will have the telepathic abilities, but your purpose is not to write books. Maybe you are to teach that these abilities are available for anyone. I believe that we all carry these different attributes and when our contract emphasizes a different one that is the one we develop more and create with.

A: Thank you; I had not thought of it as following your contract.

Q: *Yes, and a contract can always be modified with the help of your guides and teachers.*

We are at the end of our interview, and I want to thank you for your descriptions and explanations of your journey. I appreciate your coming and being a subject for this book. This is Chapter 10 so you are the last subject—a nice ending for my book. The concluding Chapter 11 will be by one of the Ascended Lady Masters.

A: I have been delighted to be here. I thank you so much. It has been great fun, better than baking a bunch of cookies.

(Chuckles) Oh, thank you; I think everything has its purpose in its place. What would we do without our chocolate chip cookies? (Laughing) Again, thank you for coming. May God bless you, and have a wonderful life and experience ahead of you.

A: Thank you, dear Author; thank you.

You are most welcome.

All right, dear one, you have done it!

Yes, I have done it. I will type this up and look forward to our concluding chapter.

Until we meet again, precious one, I AM Jeshua ben Joseph.

8:00 AM.

11 MASTER LADY NADA

1 1-26-15 Chapter 11 at 6:50 AM Thanksgiving Day.

Hello, precious one; Happy Thanksgiving to you!

Oh, thank you, Jeshua (chuckles).

All right; we are all set to bring in the very last chapter of this sequel: *Transitions, Vol. II.* The presenter will be an Ascended Lady Master. I will let her introduce herself.

Hello, my precious one; I am known as Lady Nada.

Oh hello, Lady; I have not spoken to you for a long time.

That is true; as you know, I am the twin flame of Sananda. *Yes*; so it is appropriate that I come now to conclude the last chapter of this sequel. In the previous book, he told about his death in Chapter 11, and now since this book is all about women, I come forth to tell you about mine.

You know it is not all that different for an Ascended Master to have his or her death from those on Earth. It all depends on what stage you are in for your evolution. If you already are a Master, you could be burned at the stake, crucified, or experience any of those other horrible deaths. Or you could just decide when it was time for you to vacate your body and go forward—that is what I chose to do. Not very many people know this, but I had a very lovely body. I was somewhat reluctant to leave it, but I had had it for many years—longer than the average woman would have had on Earth. I simply said that I must get on with my evolving. So I laid down and closed my eyes for the last time.

Now since I had planned this, all of my closest friends, and we will say, relatives, were with me and supporting me. They could see through the veils, you see. To them it was not a particular goodbye, for they could pop in and out of different dimensions without any effort also. So I laid down and made the transition into another dimension that you would call *death*, but we would just call *evolution* going forward.

Then there is the decision as to what to do with the body you have just vacated. You can build a funeral pyre and put the body on the logs and fire it up. You see, when you have a beautiful body, you do need to watch over it when it is dead in order to see that it is buried, if that is your wish, or cremated, or disposed of in a respectable, loving way. So there were legions of Angels guarding my dead body.

Arch Angel Michael was helping me and, of course, Sananda was there. It was decided that the cleanest way for the body was to practice how the people do it in India.

It was a very beautiful body. The body has its own Entity that we call the *Genetic Entity*. I had removed that. Therefore, basically it was just a human-like doll. I had removed all of my energy out of the body. I removed all of the memory out of those cells. Basically the body was just a blank slate on the inside.

We even created our own fire for the pyre. There are many things that Masters can do. So we all stood and concentrated bringing fire to those logs that held the body. As the flames burst upward in their own way, they devoured this beautiful, lifeless shell of my body.

Now, did I feel some grief? Yes, of course. Again, think of it in terms of having a living doll that is destroyed. So there is a loss there. There is always a loss when you have occupied a living body—a loss to the soul when he or she no longer has that body.

I think people forget the teaching, *as above, so below.* I believe that that is applicable in everything that you do and experience—your emotions, for one. Well, the Masters still have emotions, *as above.* Therefore, humanity will have its emotions, *as below.* There is an adjustment period that the Master needs to go through also, you see.

Readers who have gotten this far in our book know that one of the steps after death is to go to the Care Center to be healed. Now, the Care Center is multidimensional. You could think of it as having floors like in a hospital. You are on this floor or that floor or the 144th floor. The Masters are healed also by sound, Light, colors, and rest. They need adjustments in their energy bodies. The Care Center certainly is the hospital in the sky. There are healers who greet you. You are taken to your room that has colors of your choosing. My colors are the aquamarines, the seafoam colors. Everything is to the taste of the person who comes to be healed. I will not call the person a *patient,* for that is a different mind-set, is it not? The healing of spiritual bodies is done in the alternative way.

Time, as you know it on Earth, is not the same in Heaven. So all I can tell you is I spent time resting, meditating with my thoughts. I was allowed visitors, of course. There are no rules pertaining to visitors. Therefore, my dear twin Sananda was with me. We talked of many things: how we would continue guiding humanity. He could see my energy. He could see that the fringes looked a little frazzled—like a bad hair day. He could see edges that looked as if a flame had frizzled them here and there. So all the different energy layers were revealed and healed.

Now readers, you know what is coming up. Yes, we do have the Review of our past journey. I think humanity thinks a Review is like a sentence given by a judge—a punishment. But I assure you that is not the case. It is a learning process. The higher you evolve up Jacob's ladder, the lessons are different. They are more intense. If you harm anyone deliberately, the pain you will feel is excruciating.

There is a monitoring screen that takes you through that lifetime, no matter how many years. But you see, everyone who sits at his or her Review really wants adjustments. What helps you to decide what the adjustment will be is the feeling that you will get. You feel the hurt from somebody. And when you feel that spark of energy that is not quite right, you say, *oh yes, that needs to be adjusted. I need to do this; or I need to do that. I need to speak with my mentor or my advisor.* And yes, we have those also. Many times the advisors are the Arch Angels. I work closely with Arch Angel (AA) Michael.

After we Masters, or I have had the Review, there is a time when we meet as a group. We all know each other. Members in that group just pour their love into whoever is coming through a transition. Again, keep in mind that it is not a death we are talking about. As masters, you have already done that physical reality many times.

We sit in a circle and they mentor you. The highest evolved Beings who could possibly be, even God Himself, mentor the group. You see, we are all One. We all need adjustments at times. Never be so proud that you cannot accept a loving...you have a term *constructive... criticism.* We do not think in those terms. *This is what I see, Nada— what you were struggling with, Nada.* Now, when you approach it this way, do you see the difference, readers? If it is a physical experience in some way, it shows up on the screen again. Therefore, you can visually see a different approach to something.

So we do not feel as if someone is accusing us. These are friends and mentors of the very highest degree. They share some of their experiences. You can still say, *as above, so below.* There is no experience under the sun that someone at the highest level or at the lowest level has not experienced. It is just the application that can change. What worked with one problem will have to be adjusted, for it will not work for solving the next problem. You have to change it.

Therefore, you sit there with your mentors. It is a wonderful gathering of love. Love is just pouring onto you. Some of the Masters have had excruciating transitions. Others have just laid down and left their bodies like my dear twin. I do not believe that most humans would be able to tolerate the vibration in that room. Again, it is the intensity, you see.

Now, the reader may be wondering, *all right, you have been to the Care Center and now you have done the Group Processing. The next thing is the accommodations. What happens there?* We Masters can co-create beautiful areas that become our retreat. One familiar with most readers would be *Shamballa* in the Gobi desert, which when it was created was not a desert. It was beautifully lush gardens.

Since Sananda is my twin flame, we have our own oasis. We do not speak about it all that much or humanity would go out and try to find it. Some things are best just left alone (*smiles*). It is a sanctuary for Sananda and me and for whomever else we wish to be with us. You must be invited to come to a Master's retreat. And if you do not have that invitation, you will not be able to find it. If in some way you did find it, you would not be able to enter, for it has a force field around it that protects it. You'd be surprised in the higher dimensions how the dark forces are always peeking around hither and yon to see what mischief they can get into.

Now, dear Author, do you wish a Questions and Answers section?

Yes, but I am kind of at a loss as to what to ask you.

Questions (Q) and Answers (A)

Q: *Sananda had me asking the different subjects do you love yourself. So I will ask you that Lady Nada, do you love yourself.*

A: Oh, precious one, even we struggle with that sometimes. You are very wise to ask that question. Masters can slip, you see, which lowers their vibrations. That will show up in the Review and that will be a subject for healing and mentoring. When that happens, and it happened to me, I did not love myself. If I had loved myself, I would not have stepped off my path. At least that is how I see it now.

But I did step off my path and it hurt many people. It hurt my beloved Sananda (*she is near tears.*). I had to go through all of that in my Review and in my group mentoring. It was very painful, but you see, there is joy that comes out of that. You have so many friends to help you—not only your loving twin but the Angels and the mentoring group, as you strive to regain the higher vibration that you once had. I now love myself, but at one time, or I will say at that time, I did not.

Q: *Thank you, Lady Nada, for your honesty. Another question I will ask (I had not asked the others, for I had not thought about it.), are some people actually descended from Angels, the Cherubim? Since you and Sananda are twin flames, twin souls, I will ask, are you Cherubim?*

A: Yes, dear one, I am, as is Jeshua/Sananda. We were created by God. All the Cherubim were. It becomes a huge soul group and that is all I need to say. Many of humanity are Cherubim, as you are, dear Author. *Oh boy, I have puzzled over that.*

Q: *I am thinking what else I could ask you. I would like to know and for the readers, since you have had bodies on Earth, what you believe is the most important lesson for humanity to learn?*

A: That is an easy question to answer. They need to learn how to love unconditionally. While that is an easy answer, it is a very complicated journey. So many people do not have the true concept of what love is—absolute unconditional love. That is what my flame has for me and I for him. There is no right or wrong in our belief systems. There is only a love that can see different ways of being.

If you do something this way, this is the consequence. If you do something in another way, that will be the consequence. Which consequence do you feel would be best for you at this time—unconditional?

Mothers will love their children, but many mothers do not love the child unconditionally. Human mothers have a way of loving their sons in a possessive way. That is not unconditional. It almost becomes... let me see how I can say this...in the Animal Kingdom, a mother cat—a tiger—protects her young with an awesome fierceness. Yet, for humanity, that fierceness could be described as love. *Do not hurt or do harm to my baby.* Then, through the years, that love must have its own dimensions—its own flexibility. If a child goes down a dark path, the mother loves the child fiercely. Then, if she is able, she will do everything she can to help the child choose a better way of walking its path.

Do you feel, Author, that this is a good time for me to make our concluding statement?

Yes, I was thinking that also, Lady.

Readers, this book is completed. The theme here for the deaths and the entrance to Heaven is to take out the fears you may have over dying. Most people fear death because it can be so painful. They are more afraid of the painful finality, like a car wreck or murder. If they did not have that, there would not be so much fear.

You have heard people say, *I wish I could close my eyes, sleep and wake up dead.* In fact, there are those who do not know they have died (*One of our subjects will attest to that.*). Then there is the entrance into

Heaven and all the things you have been wondering about—healing, Review, and what the Author calls the *Group Processing.*

So the purpose of these two books is to educate you and to alleviate your fears, so that when the time comes for your death that was in your contract and you had agreed to, all is well. Your Heaven is a beautiful place with many dimensions and realms. I think a good idea to embrace is that most things are not as simple as they look to be. You thought of Heaven as being just a place in the sky. Now you are finding out it is multidimensional and just magnificent—beyond anything you may have dreamed or seen in the movies. As the saying goes, *it will blow your mind.*

I AM Lady Nada, and I bless you readers. I hope my words will hold a deep meaning for you. We can all heal from our diversities and become the stronger for them. Namaste.

Lady Nada, thank you for your honesty and wisdom. I am honored that you came to tell us your story and to close this book. My deepest love and appreciation to you and Jeshua/Sananda. 8:00 AM.

EPILOGUE

November 28, 2015, Saturday. This sequel, BOOK 14, took longer than I had anticipated. I channeled the last chapter on Thanksgiving Day and finished transcribing it today. (I immediately forwarded it on to my editor, Heather Clarke.)

On June 23, 2015, I underwent an operation on my right eye. I have Glaucoma and I needed a new bleb (no that is not a typo) as the one I had was leaking profusely, causing considerable irritation to my eye. Of course I lost all incentive to write my book. (When you cannot see out of one eye due to the irritation and leakage, any inclination to use the eye for other than to see to get around is quickly put on the back burner.)

My life was totally focused on doctor appointments, when to use what drops and so forth. Gradually, my eye trauma settled down; the pressures were in the high teens, although the steady eye drop therapy continues as the doctor would like to see them lower.

Now I can get back to my book, I mused to myself. The women came forth as if they had not been waiting their turns. And I carried on. I have read the chapters over and even I would look forward to each new chapter with anticipation. I was struck by the level of evolution by these women. Most all had joined their soul groups which shows a growth in their development.

People always ask about my next book. At present, I do not feel a new theme germinating on the back burner. However, I have learned to never say *never*. It is up to my Higher Self to reveal what it has for my future endeavor.

I am so appreciative of your interest in my books, readers. Please contact me at <u>azchako@aol.com</u> and/or <u>www.Godumentary.com/chako</u> for your comments.

My love and blessings to all, Chako
12-01-15

ACKNOWLEDGEMENTS

There is so much to be grateful for: I owe so much gratitude to all of my women subjects who came forth so willingly to tell me and the readers their death journey and their entrance into Heaven. Without them, there would be no book!

I thank Heather Clarke for her expertise in editing the various chapters in a timely fashion. She kept the book flowing forth and diligently watched for excess commas.

Jeshua/ Jesus/Sananda is my gate keeper and I thank him for bringing such an interesting group of women for this sequel.

God, the Ascended Masters, and Angels all helped me stay grounded and cleared of the subjects' energies when the interviews were completed. I am deeply grateful for their expertise which helped me to confidently greet each of my subjects, to interview them, and to say goodbye to them.

And I also thank Trafford Publishing for the wonderful service they provide us self-publishing Authors.

My deepest gratitude and love to all…

12-03-15

LIST OF PREVIOUS BOOKS

Verling CHAKO Priest, Ph.D.

The Ultimate Experience, the Many Paths to God series:
BOOKS 1, 2, & 3 REVISITED (2011)
ISBN # 978-1-4269-7664-3 (sc)
ISBN# 978-1-4269-7665-0 (e-book)
REALITIES of the CRUCIFIXION (2006)
ISBN # 1-978-4669-2148-1
MESSAGES from the HEAVENLY HOSTS (2007)
ISBN # 1-4251-2550-6
YOUR SPACE BROTHERS and SISTERS GREET
YOU! (2008) ISBN # 978-1-4251-6302-0
TEACHINGS of the MASTERS of LIGHT (2008)
ISBN # 978-1-4251-8573-2
PAULUS of TARSUS (2010)
ISBN # 978-1-4669-209-1 (sc)
ISBN # 978-1-4669-2090-3 (e-book)
THE GODDESS RETURNS to EARTH (2010)
ISBN # 978-1-4269-3563-3
ISBN # 978-1-4269-3564-0 (e-book)
JESUS: MY BELOVED CONNECTION TO
HUMANITY AND THE SEA Revised Edition (2013)
CO-AUTHOR REV. CYNTHIA WILLIAMS
ISBN # 978-1-4669-7641-2(sc)
ISBN # 978-1-4669-7642-9(hc)

Verling Chako Priest, Ph.D.

ISBN # 978-1-4669-7640-5(e)

MASTERS' TALES of NOW (2013)

ISBN #978-1-4907-1351-9 (sc)

ISBN #978-4907-1350-2 (hc)

ISBN #978-1-4907-1352-6 (e-book)

RELATIONSHIPS (2014)

ISBN #978-1-4907-5188-7 (sc)

#978 1 4907-5190-0 (hc)

#978-1-4907-5189-4 (e)

TRANSITIONS (2015)

ISBN #978-1-4907-5836-7 (sc)

#978-1-4907-5838-1 (hc)

#978-1-4907-5837-4 (e)

TRANSITIONS Vol. II (2015)

ISBN # Pending

Available at Trafford: 1-888-232-4444

Or, Amazon.com

www.godumentary.com/chako.

READER'S NOTES

ABOUT THE AUTHOR

Verling (CHAKO) Priest, PhD was born in Juneau, Alaska, hence her name of Cheechako, shortened to just Chako by her mother, a medical doctor, and her father, an Orthodontist. Chako was raised in Napa, CA. She attended the University of California at Berkeley where she met her future husband. Upon their marriage and after his training as a Navy pilot, they settled into the military way of life. They lived twelve years outside of the United States Mainland in various places, which included Hawaii, Viet Nam, Australia, and Greece. Little did she know that these exotic lands and peoples were preparing her for her spiritual awakening years hence?

After her husband's retirement from the Navy, they resettled in Napa, California. It was during this time that she returned to school at Berkeley, transferred to Sonoma University where she earned her first two degrees in Psychology. Chako then entered the doctoral program at the Institute of Transpersonal Psychology (ITP), renamed Sufi University, which is now located in Palo Alto, CA. She successfully completed that program which consisted of a Master, as well as the Doctorate in Transpersonal Psychology. Ten years and four degrees later she was able to pursue her passion for Metaphysical and New Age Thought—her introduction into the realm of the Spiritual Hierarchy and the Ascended Lords and Masters.

In 1988, Dr. Priest moved to Minnetonka, Minnesota. She co-authored a program called, *Second Time Around* for those with recurring cancer for Methodist Hospital. She, as a volunteer, also facilitated a grief group for Pathways of Minneapolis, and had a private practice.

She studied with a spiritual group in Minnetonka led by Donna Taylor and the Teacher, a group of 5 highly developed entities trance-channeled by Donna. The group traveled extensively all over the world working with the energy grids of the planet and regaining parts of their energies that were still in sacred areas waiting to be reclaimed by them, the owners. They climbed in and out of the pyramids in Egypt, tromped through the Amazon forest in Venezuela, rode camels at Sinai, and climbed the Mountain. Hiked the paths at Qumran, trod the ancient roadways in Petra, Jordan, and walked where the Master Yeshua/Jesus walked in Israel.

The time came, November 1999, when Chako was guided to move to Arizona—her next period of growth. This is where she found her beloved Masters, who in reality had always been with her. They were **all** ready for her next phase, bringing into the physical many books—mind-provoking books, telepathically received by her, from these highly evolved, beautiful, loving Beings. Each book stretches her capabilities, as well as her belief systems. Nevertheless, it is a challenge she gladly embraces.

It is now April, 03, 2015. She has finished writing her thirteenth book, *TRANSITIONS: Death Processes & Beyond of 11 Entities.* Blessings!

Comments to
azchako@aol.com

Godumentary.com/chako

CPSIA information can be obtained at www.ICGtesting.com
Printed in the USA
LVOW06*2044150116

469920LV00004B/7/P